'John Haldane offers a provoc...religion as "not only credible but necessary" and is ... grapple with the problems now raised by religious fundamentalism ... Haldane's reading in philosophy and theology is astounding'

The Obs...er

'Haldane is a distinguished philosopher and a strong believer in explanation ... this book fulfils its stated purpose admirably, which was to give us reason to believ

'[Haldane] aims "to confront proper role to play in the in sounds, spiritual life of educat... firm he challenges secular triumphalism'

Times Literary Supplement

'Elegantly written, lucid and logically constructed'

The Independent

'Remarkable for its deft interweaving of current affairs with a lucid and convincing explanation of how religion provides an overarching account of the meaning of human existence ... This guide is intelligent, but it is also disarmingly down to earth'

Church Times

'What has almost disappeared is the traditional Catholic portrayal of faith as consistent with, indeed as the perfection of, reason. *An Intelligent Person's Guide to Religion* is a lucid and timely restatement of this classic position ... a worthy book'

New Statesman

An Intelligent Person's Guide to Religion

John Haldane

Duckworth Overlook
London · New York · Woodstock

200
HAL

This edition 2005
First published in 2003 by
Duckworth Overlook

LONDON
90-93 Cowcross Street
London EC1M 6BF
inquiries@duckworth-publishers.co.uk
www.ducknet.co.uk

NEW YORK
The Overlook Press
141 Wooster Street
New York, NY 10012

WOODSTOCK
The Overlook Press
One Overlook Drive
Woodstock, NY 12498
www.overlookpress.com
[for individual orders and bulk sales in the United States,
please contact our Woodstock office]

A CIP catalogue record for this book is available from the
British Library and the Library of Congress

ISBN 0 7156 3376 7 (UK)
ISBN 1-58567-722-1 (US)

Typeset by E-Type, Liverpool
Printed and bound in Great Britain by
CPD Ltd, Wales

Contents

In memory of James and Hilda Haldane
who loved and were loved
more deeply than words can convey

Preface

This book is a contribution to the discussion of the place of religion in human life. It is addressed to a readership that will include committed believers, assured atheists, and confirmed agnostics. I suspect it will also include some who, though not quite agnostic, are uncertain about the religion they practise, and others who, though without a faith, speculate that there may be a God. I doubt, however, that there will be any readers who are wholly indifferent to the matter of religion. Yet there do appear to be such people. This is something of a puzzle to me. I can appreciate that what exercises the imagination, reason and passion of some may leave others untouched; but that *religion* should be a subject of indifference raises questions about the orientation of such people's lives. Religion engages our intelligence at two levels. First, with questions of particular and immediate religious truth, meaning, feeling and practice. Second, with more general and abstract issues about the truth of religion and the significance of religious hope and fear. It is more understandable, I think, that someone should be indifferent to the particular and the immediate, but to care nothing for the second set of issues would suggest at least a want of reflective curiosity, and perhaps a failure of existential engagement.

I have approached the general topic, and the specific aspects signalled by the chapter titles, in ways designed to engage those for whom questions of the existence of God, the meaning of life, and the contribution of religion are significant. But I hope that if someone indifferent to these matters were persuaded to read this book, then he or she might complete it thinking that, after all, this is an area in which an intelligent person should aim to form a view. As a philosopher I aim to answer questions of truth, meaning and value. That involves assessing the coherence and cogency of various ideas, and presenting arguments in support of definite conclusions. Not all considerations pro and con can be reduced to abstract formulations, however; nor is it reasonable to expect any significant conclusion to be beyond dispute. Such is the nature of the subject matter, and such, perhaps, is our human condition.

In a short novel, *A Corner of the Veil* (1999), Laurence Cosse imagines that a member of the French province of a religious order, the 'Casuists' (Jesuits?), receives a short manuscript containing a clear and incontrovertible demonstration of the existence of God. Besides having the merit of establishing the case beyond any possible doubt, the form of the proof also solves the mystery of why a good God would permit evil. Though it is never clearly specified, there are hints to suggest that the answer is that everything is as it *must* be, and that God is intimately present in all that happens, thereby making it to be good however else it may appear. At any rate, the effect of reading the proof is to provide immediate conviction of the existence of God, of his goodness and of the meaning of life: 'Believing was no longer an issue. The world was intelligible. Ears heard: cacophony was gone from creation. Eyes saw: the universe, hitherto jumbled like a holographic drawing, now found its depth and meaning.' The recipient of the letter is the editor of a prominent journal, *Outlooks*, and the issue of publication arises. Before a decision can be made, however, the editor shares the letter with a fellow Casuist who has been working on a book that aims to show that the existence of God cannot possibly be proved. He, too, is utterly convinced, as are others in turn. What follows is a narrative of intended revelation and attempted concealment involving senior members of the Casuists, the French Government and the Vatican. The presiding issue is whether it is in the interests of these parties and of the world in general to know what the proof shows.

Cosse's story begs some questions but raises others. It is not credible to think that there could be a proof of the existence of God that was entirely beyond doubt or even question. It is unlikely, even were there such, that it would be taken up much beyond academic circles, and certainly it is hard to believe that politicians would rush to consider how to deal with the matter. It is, however, interesting to speculate how, if the issues of God's existence and of the meaning of life were to be demonstrated beyond doubt, this would impact on human existence. Would one go to bed following such a day of discovery feeling informed but otherwise unchanged? Would one spend the night in private devotion, or gather with neighbours for a street party, or drink to celebrate or blot out the revelation? Would following days take their customary course? Would one want to live patiently awaiting eternity or to rush headlong into it? The truth about religion is not without practical implications. Indeed, the issues it addresses are as much 'existential' as speculative. It will become apparent where I stand on some of these matters, but readers will bring their own thoughts to the text and take their own conclusions away from it. One day, perhaps, we may each know what for now we can only wonder about; in the meantime we should at least strive to deepen our understanding.

The idea of this book was first conceived by Robin Baird Smith. Since I received the commission, my efforts to write it have been subject to unavoidable delays and interruptions. During that period I have benefited from the encouragement and patience of staff at Duckworth: first of Martin Rynja and then of Deborah Blake. To them, to Robin Baird Smith and most recently to Eleanor Birne, I offer many thanks. Most of the writing was done while I held the Royden Davis Chair of Humanities at Georgetown University in Washington, and I am grateful to the University for an appointment that provided ample opportunity for thinking and writing. Scientists require equipment and materials; philosophers ask only for time and the wisdom of other minds. Georgetown was generous in the former regard, and I was very fortunate to have the critical responses, chapter by chapter, of Dr William Haines of its Department of Philosophy. There is much in what follows with which he would still disagree, but his comments on previous versions were generously given, invariably helpful, and gratefully received.

The writing of this book and similar activities have long been met with enormous patience and support from my family, who deserve better, but who, I hope, may nevertheless think my time and energies were spent in a worthwhile cause. It has often been said that one motive for religious belief is the hope of enjoying for ever the company of those whom one loves. There is surely something in this suggestion, and the hope is not, I believe, altogether vain. Whatever the truth about eternity, however, for now I offer this book with my deepest love and gratitude to my wife Hilda and to my children Kirsty, James, Alice and John.

Introduction

Said Waldershare, 'Sensible men are all of the same religion.'
'And pray what is that?' … 'Sensible men never tell.'
Benjamin Disraeli

There is no such thing as 'religion in general', any more
than there is any such creature as an 'animal in general'.
Every animal is of some or other species, and each has its
own distinguishing marks. So, too, every religion is characterised by its founding myths, its sacred scriptures, its
dogmas and doctrines, its codes and commandments, its
rituals and sacraments, its deities and demons. Every
faith has its contrasting denominations, sects and tendencies. A few years ago I was visiting a university in
Southern California and wanted to find out what churches
there were in the area. Having found nothing in the
vicinity of the university, I stopped at a garage forecourt
and borrowed a telephone directory. Very quickly I
discovered page upon page of entries for churches, by
which I mean not just different places of worship but
different faiths and denominations. It is said that there are
over 20,000 different Christian denominations alone, and
for all I know it may well be that half of these are represented in California. Additionally, the United States is

home to a vast array of faiths and cults, reflecting, perhaps uniquely within the confines of a single state, the religious diversity of the wider world. An admittedly crude measure of that diversity is the fact that around the globe there are now over nine thousand distinct and separate religions, with a hundred or so new ones coming into being every year.

Abstract generalised discussion of religion is thus liable to suffer a fate analogous to that of generalised, non-credal religious education which, in its British state-school manifestation, was once described as 'the religion of nobody taught by anybody and paid for by everybody'. As practised in schools such education fails to the extent that it either confronts children of different backgrounds with beliefs which they do not hold, or else fails to instruct them about what they and their families do believe – and often it is culpable on both counts. (Such, indeed, is the ground advanced by Christians, Jews and Muslims for having their own schools.) Similarly, a survey guide to religion which did not adopt the policy of providing an introduction to the history, beliefs and practices of different faiths but sought instead to introduce the reader to 'religion in general' would be liable to be similarly flawed.

Besides being intellectually suspect, focusing on religion in general can result in a kind of spiritual journeying which, far from being a serious pursuit of religious truth, is more akin to tourism. In Victorian and Edwardian times there was a limited fashion for experimenting with various religions, usually moving from some species of Christianity through Eastern religions or 'oriental cults' to one or other form of syncretism, often with a markedly 'spiritualist' character. Though this once seemed quite the most radical experimentalism, and was denounced by clergymen as liable to lead practitioners out of their minds and into that of the Devil, it seems staid by standards now established among 'spiritual seekers' in North America. The author of one text recounts how, following a near-death experience, she began a religious search that led her first to Lutheranism and from there to taking spiritual direction from native Americans, from a Hassidic Jewish Rabbi, American yoga and Buddhist teachers, a Sufi master, a German Roman Catholic monk, Russian Orthodox monks, 'Scotch mystics' (*sic*), a Korean Taoist master and, most recently, a Sikh visionary in whose Indian community the religious festivals of all faiths are celebrated.

No doubt such wide-ranging travels broaden the mind, but it does not follow that they produce any deeper appreciation of the meaning and value of religion than would be achieved by staying within a single faith tradition, exploring its teachings and practices and then, if this should seem pointful, identifying parallels and counterparts in other faiths. Certainly in the educational case the wise policy is to explore religion from the perspective of some particular faith or tradition, encouraging in due course extrapolation and the drawing of analogies between the structure and substance of one religion and those of others.

The present exercise, however, is not primarily an educational one. This book is not a student text or a layman's introduction as those are generally understood – though I hope students and general readers will find it stimulating. Its purpose is rather one of engaged, broadly philosophical, exploration of the position of religion in the contemporary world. A survey of the religious studies shelves of a well-stocked bookshop will reveal a number of good introductions to world faiths and particular denominations, and to different approaches to the study of religion – anthropological, historical, philosophical, psychological, sociological, theological and so on – as well as to its various aspects: the doctrinal, the mystical, the organisational, the ritualistic, etc. There is a plentiful supply of good introductions and scholarly monographs, and I am not aiming here to add to either category. Instead, I wish to confront the suggestion that religion has no proper role to play in the intellectual, moral and – odd though it sounds – spiritual life of educated and intelligent persons.

That the claims of religion to explain the existence and character of the world are undermined by science is now a common idea, owing principally to (certain interpretations of) advances in physics and biology. That the role of religion as a source of moral guidance has been subverted is also a familiar notion thanks to psychology, sociology and the emergence of secular ethics. Times must have been hard, however, for priests, ministers, imams, rabbis, and their other-faith counterparts when news came through of 'post-religious spiritualities'. Yet this is precisely the status claimed by various new age theories and practices, and no doubt their influence is part of the reason why in Western societies more people are now said to believe in the soul or spirit than to believe in God.

Scholars have wearied themselves, their students and their readers in trying to define religion. The basic problem is avoiding an account that is too narrow, while also avoiding a definition that is so broad as to fail to capture any distinctive character. Older dictionary definitions of religion, fashioned in less culturally pluralistic times, typically refer to 'a belief in, and worship of, a god or gods'. These specifications fail in the first respect. Recent writers aware of the large array of 'belief systems' sometimes favour definitions couched in terms of 'a commitment to a perspective of ultimate and universal value', but this is clearly too broad – if not, indeed, quaintly vacuous. Another tendency is to present one's own favoured theory of religious motivation or value as if it were a definition of the very phenomenon. This sometimes results in quite eccentric and contradictory accounts, as in the philosopher Alfred North Whitehead's observation that religion is 'what the individual does with his own solitude' and the sociologist Emile Durkheim's dictum that religion 'is an eminently collective thing'.

It is tempting to trace these suggestions to the professional preoccupations of their authors, for while philosophers spend a good deal of time on their own working out ideas, sociologists and social anthropologists occupy themselves watching others living out social practices. To the extent that a general definition seems called for, religion is best characterised as a system of beliefs and practices directed towards a transcendent reality in relation to which persons seek solutions to the observed facts of moral and physical evil, limitation and vulnerability, particularly and especially death. As well as abstract and general classification, however, there is also the alternative of ostensive definition – that is, pointing to cases of the phenomenon in question. Admittedly this has the limitation that having recognised one or several examples one may yet not have the means of determining other cases. Yet the claim to 'know one when one sees one' is not vacuous either. It is, after all, how most of us proceed most of the time and its general success is not in doubt.

In the West we are familiar with a range of major religions that are united around certain basic philosophical/theological ideas, the general term for which is 'theism'. By 'religion', this is what I shall have in mind, unless indicated otherwise – e.g. in relation to Buddhism, Hinduism and 'new age religions', which are generally not of this sort. Theism is the belief in a single, all-knowing, all-good, all-present and all-powerful, eternally existing God who created and sustains the universe. More specifically I shall have in mind the so-called 'Abrahamic faiths' or 'religions of the book': Judaism, Christianity and Islam. These descriptions derive, first, from the account given in the Torah (the first five books of the Hebrew Bible, by tradition ascribed to Moses) of God's promise to Abraham 'I will bless you ... and by you all the families of the Earth shall bless themselves' (Genesis 12:3); and, second, from the fact that all three religions recognise the authority of the Hebrew Bible as the word of God to humankind. The differences between them reside in what else they do or do not accept as revelation, and in what they take to follow from this.

Yet more precisely, the perspective from which I will be viewing the challenge that religion is otiose is a Judaeo-Christian one; since, ironically, it is principally within societies which once occupied this perspective that the charges of its redundancy, irrelevance and falsity are most often brought. The issues, however, are more general, and anyone interested in the intellectual and moral position of religion in the infancy of the third millennium, particularly if they are positively disposed to or even just open-minded about faith, will, I hope, find themselves stimulated by what follows, and perhaps even persuaded by it.

1

Religion and the Prophets of Doom

The simple believes everything,
but the prudent looks where he is going.
Proverbs

The state of religion in the contemporary world is curiously paradoxical. Sociologists studying advanced technological societies have long been taken with the idea of secularisation, and have continued for some generations to pronounce the fatal condition of religion. They now seem equally happy, however, to go on conducting surveys into the state of belief, and to report that religious ideas show little sign of fading away. Indeed, a second phase of the sociology of religion has made much of the rise of fundamentalism, focusing mostly on non-Western contexts, such as the Middle East, India and Asia, and when directing its attention to the West, restricting the phenomenon to 'less sophisticated' populations. Yet more recently it has become fashionable to study new religious movements ('NRMs') and to observe the remarkable growth of these, and the fact that in the West especially they tend to attract the young, well-educated and relatively affluent. Any appearance of contradiction in these analyses is avoided by distinguishing between organised and traditional faiths on the one hand, and religious feelings and aspirations on the other. Indeed, it becomes possible to argue that the very process of secularisation has made space for new movements to develop and flourish.

This only serves to deepen the puzzle of religion. If people no longer attend the synagogues, churches, mosques and temples of their parents and grandparents, why do they persist in believing in the transcendent, engaging in petitionary prayer and hoping for life beyond the grave? For there is little reason to believe in, practise and hope for these things, save on the basis of a more or less traditional faith. Certainly, the members of the Heaven's Gate and Solar Temple communities shared beliefs about imminent transportation into the beyond, but the evident absurdity of their blends of science fiction and modern occultism was an obvious factor in their collective suicides. Traditional religions are more reconciled to the ordinariness of life, and where they were deeply settled their influence persists. One recent survey conducted by the Centre for Sociological Research in Spain produced the interesting result that more people defined themselves as Catholics than claimed to believe in God (84 and 77 per cent respectively). This appeared to echo on a national level the state of mind Bertrand Russell attributed to the Spanish-American philosopher George Santayana when he wrote: 'Santayana believes that there is no God and that his [God's] mother's name is Mary.'

Any tendency to dismiss this result as demonstrating no more than Latin sentimentalism has to take account of the fact that in Britain and in the less committedly religious parts of North America attitudes seem similarly ambiguous. A survey commissioned from Gallup in 1999 by the *Daily Telegraph* to assess the state of Christianity in Britain on the eve of the new millennium produced such results as that 15 per cent of those describing themselves as Christians also said they did not believe in God, and 39 per cent of the same 'Christians' said they did not believe in life after death. The first result is in fact less paradoxical than the Spanish one, since Britain is a more ethnically and religiously diverse country and it is likely that in identifying themselves as 'Christian' some respondents only meant to indicate that they were not Jews, Muslims, Hindus, Sikhs and so on. Additionally, the term 'Christian' carries a note of thoughtfulness and social concern that some may be happy to be associated with, even though they have no relevant religious beliefs.

More significantly, perhaps, the most recent and most extensive poll of British moral and religious dispositions (commissioned from Opinion Research in 2000 by the BBC in connection with a nine-part television series on *The Soul of Britain*) included the result that more people believe in a soul than believe in God. Admittedly this lacks the immediately contradictory character of the Spanish Catholic atheists, and the lesser paradox of

British 'Christian' non-believers. Nonetheless, given that for the most part beliefs in an immaterial self have been strongly associated with belief in God, this degree of uncoupling has some significance. Moreover, the British trend appears to be moving in that direction, for while belief in a soul has increased in the last twenty years, belief in God has declined and has done so at a faster rate.

What is to be made of such findings? One might say that people remain attracted to religious ideas while having lost confidence in religious doctrines and institutions. But that is far too simple. For one thing many people are members of religious faiths, and within these groups there are signs of growth. Over a third of the world's population (almost two billion people) are Christians, and half of this number are Roman Catholics. The latter is a form of religion that is hardly light on dogma and doctrine, asserting as it does that God is three persons in one divinity; that one of those persons, Jesus Christ, had both human and divine natures; that his earthly mother, Mary, was herself conceived without stain of sin and became pregnant though she remained a virgin; that Christ died and rose from the dead; that he bestowed powers of infallibility on a church; and that, through the actions of a priest, bread and wine are changed into the glorified flesh and blood of the risen Christ.

Another traditional and dogmatic religion is Islam, itself with more than a billion adherents. According to the Muslim faith there is but one God, Allah, to whose will – as dictated to the Prophet Mohammed by the angel

Gabriel and recorded in the Qur'an (Koran) – all must surrender. Allah is 'most gracious and most merciful' and will reward those who live by the five pillars of Islam – witnessing to the faith, ritual prayer, *zakat* (obligatory charity), *hajj* (pilgrimage to Mecca) and fasting during the month of Ramadan. But those who fail to heed the call will be punished in the afterlife. For all that Islam may seem to be at odds with the scientific and moral outlook of the contemporary age, there are almost as many Muslims in the world as there are non-religious people, and many of those Muslims now live in advanced industrial societies, including Western ones. Within a generation, for example, Islam will be the second largest faith in the United States (itself a highly churched society). Indeed, globally, the religious outnumber agnostics and atheists by four to one.

Additionally and unsurprisingly, committed believers tend to be better informed than non-believers about religious ideas, their meanings and their implications. This makes it difficult to interpret the finding that almost 70 per cent of those recently polled in Britain believe in a soul, while fewer than 30 per cent believe in a personal God. A traditional Christian is likely to maintain that the soul is an immaterial entity or principle, infused into the body by God in order that it might pursue a course on Earth that will lead, good-living and God-willing, to eternal life with other redeemed souls and with their Creator in Heaven. Later I shall discuss the viability of these ideas, but for now the point to observe is that they fit together as interconnected elements in a broad religious picture. How so the ideas of those who believe in a soul but not in God? What do they think a soul is? Where do they think it comes from? How do they think it is possible that there should be immaterial selves in a Godless universe? What do they think happens to souls when bodies die? What do they make of eternity? Pollsters rarely, if ever, ask such questions, but unless we know what people really do and do not believe, then claims about the religious condition of society based on such surveys do not add up to very much. Neither those who maintain that we are moving into a post-dogmatic age, nor those who assert that spirituality is undiminished, can claim a great deal in the way of definite or hard evidence from standard opinion polls.

In fact, the relationship between surveys of opinion and sociological/intellectual conjectures of religious decline is probably the reverse of what it is usually supposed to be. Polls do not form the basis of a scientific assessment: the secularist thought has tended to be father to the sociological deed. Over the course of a century or so, the view has been formed and disseminated that religious metaphysics has been subverted by natural science, and that religious practice has been disclosed as self-deception or social manipulation. The result is that those shaped by a certain sort of naturalistic education, and those informed by popularising presentations of its ideas, tend to presume that traditional religion must be in decline *because it ought to be*, and so fashion and interpret surveys accordingly. An example of this presumption, typical of the secular confidence of its period, comes from an interview with the American sociologist Peter Berger who is well known for his writings on religion and modern society. Towards the end of the 1960s Berger gave an interview to the *New York Times* claiming that by 'the 21st century religious believers are likely to be found only in small sects, huddled together to resist a worldwide secular culture'. In retrospect, this prediction, from which Berger has long distanced himself, simply looks absurd. At the time, however, it seemed to many to have impeccable credentials, for the idea of inevitable religious decline followed from the general argument that modernisation and secularisation go hand in hand, and was supported by various assumptions about the redundancy of religion based on the ideas of such figures as Darwin, Freud, Nietzsche and Marx.

Surprisingly, however, this sort of naturalistic, anti-mythological thinking is also to be found among religious leaders. Most markedly among Christian denominations, Anglicanism has made something of a speciality out of episcopal heterodoxy, with senior figures – including the former Bishops David Jenkins in England, Richard Holloway in Scotland, James Spong in the US and Archbishop Peter Carnley in Australia – all questioning traditional Christian doctrines such as the bodily resurrection of Christ, the Virgin Birth, the uniqueness of Jesus as a route to salvation, and Christian teachings on sex and marriage. As interesting as what they deny, however, are the grounds given for 'revising' religious claims. In an interview with John Mortimer published in the *Sunday Times* in 1985 while he was still Bishop of Durham, Dr Jenkins restated opinions of the sort that had given offence and scandal to many devout Anglicans, and then added by way of explanation that 'miraculous claims put ordinary, sensible people off Christianity … they say "go tell that to the marines."' More recently, after being elected to the position of Primate of the Anglican Church of Australia, Archbishop Carnley wrote an article published just before Easter 2000 in which he questioned the commonly accepted interpretation of the resurrection of Jesus. He even made a point of quoting Jenkins's famous words about the 'Easter event' not being 'a conjuring trick with bones' before going on to give a version of a standard 'demythologising' account: 'Jesus reappears as the bearer of salvation in the concrete form of acceptance and forgiveness.' Similarly, Richard Holloway, following his retirement in 2001 as Primate of the Scottish Episcopal Church and Bishop of Edinburgh, remarked in an interview that 'if people could really understand that the nature of religion is [as a] wonderful mythic, symbolic, poetic system about deep truth, then they would relax. But we claim that you have to get into your head certain convictions about historical events that are in a sense irrelevant.' What all of this seems to mean is that Jesus Christ did not in fact rise from the dead and appear to his disciples and others, but that those who follow his spiritual teachings and example may be inspired to be forgiving and accepting. So much for the unambiguous words of St Paul in his First Letter to the Corinthians (15:12-15): 'Now if Christ is preached as raised from the dead, how can some of you say that there is no resurrection of the dead? ... If Christ has not been raised, then our preaching is in vain and your faith is in vain.'

Revisionist interpretations are generally motivated by an acceptance of post-Enlightenment secular ideas and by the suspicion, fear or belief that traditional Christian theology now lacks credibility. Such attitudes lie behind the comment about the miraculous putting ordinary people off Christianity to the extent of their saying 'tell that to the marines'. Similarly, James Spong has written of 'bringing Christian belief into the 21st century'; he has called for a 'new reformation', writing that 'God as a personal being with expanded supernatural human and parental qualities ... does not work [*sic*] for 21st-century Christians'; and he has commented that 'the idea of Christ as incarnation of God is bankrupt [and the Biblical creation story is] pre-Darwinian mythology and post-Darwinian nonsense'. For Bishop Holloway, the Church is 'going down the tubes' and is 'out of synch' with contemporary attitudes and values. Yet while being uttered in the hope of seeming engaged and relevant, such remarks only serve to reinforce the old image of would-be fashionable clerics seeking acceptance by talking the talk of the world and managing in the process to get everything wrong. The orthodox are scandalised, the secular are unimpressed and younger generations are bemused by a language they do not quite understand. Far from the idea of the miraculous or of God as a personal being alienating 'ordinary people', they are strongly attracted to them out of curiosity and even more so out of hope.

If ordinary people have a problem with miracles it is not because they have absorbed the philosophy of scientific materialism, but only because they have never seen one. That, of course, was one of the main points of traditional episcopal responsibility: to preach and teach the miracles testified to by the writers of the Gospels and Epistles. It was and largely still is the case that Christians believe in the divinity of Christ because of the miraculous signs recorded in scripture: 'Now Jesus did many signs in the presence of the disciples, which are not written in this book; but these are written that you may believe that Jesus is the Christ (Messiah), the Son of the Living God' (John 20:30). If the first Christians had taken the view of church leaders such as Spong, Jenkins, Holloway and Carnley, it is hard to believe that Christianity would have survived the lifetimes of the apostles. Certainly it is impossible to imagine saints and martyrs enduring all sorts of tribulations to spread the word that Jesus was simply 'an extraordinary man' and that claims as to his divinity are really 'metaphors for living a good and humane life'. Likewise, Muslims who doubt the veracity of Mohammed's proclaimed experiences of the angel Gabriel, or Jews who reject the idea that Abraham and Moses were divinely commissioned, or Hindus who regard as mere myths the traditional belief that each soul is an emanation of Brahman (the universal spirit and ulti-mate reality) to which, by observing *Dharma* (the cosmic moral/religious law), it may hope after death to be united, are certainly all destined to be overtaken by secularisation – but only because they have already begun to embrace it.

None of this establishes the truth of any religious doctrine or historical claim, but it should encourage wari-ness of attempts by religious leaders to accommodate themselves to the naturalistic, secularised thinking of those prophets of doom who proclaim the demise of tradi-tional religion and who cite opinion surveys in an effort to confirm this. What people say in response to polls about religion and morality has to be set within the context of what else they say and do, and of what they know and understand. Taken by themselves solicited affirmations or rejections of abstract propositions remain ambiguous in their meaning and uncertain in their implications.

Facts belong in contexts: just as individual colours set against variable backgrounds may appear quite different, so claims about morality and religion need to be assessed against the assumptions from which they arise. Should everyone's claim about the existence and nature of God, or of souls, or of Heaven and Hell, be treated equally when determining what society believes, or what people ought to believe? Are the claims of two people, each of whom maintains they believe in a soul, to be given equal credibility when the first has a background of traditional religious education, while the other relies on a diet of magazine stories about reincarnation and hauntings? I don't mean to ask whose belief we should treat as more likely to be true, but rather whose statement of opinion we should take more seriously as an expression of genuine belief. Suppose that in technologically advanced and prosperous societies many people's experiences have become detached from the facts of life, suffering, joy and death, and have moved from the intensity of these to the numbing blandishments of consumerism and the dumbing routine of popular television; but suppose also that through background or personal experience a smaller but more committed group have held fast to traditional religious ideas and practices. Quite generally, those who maintain beliefs *contra mundum* tend to be clearer about the matters in question than those who go with the flow.

Under the hypothesis of differential experience it becomes harder to know how to assess the 'soul of the nation', or even to know quite what to make of the idea of religious decline, other than as a decline in religious *knowledge*. Interestingly, when asked why they thought some people do not believe there is a God (meaning, I take it, why some believe there is no God), more respondents in the *Soul of Britain* poll cited 'lack of knowledge and teaching about God' (31 per cent) than supposed that 'science has explained the mysteries of life' (22 per cent), or that 'the concept of God is irrelevant to modern society' (20 per cent). This provides a context for the following results from the *Daily Telegraph* Millennium Poll. Whereas in 1949 only 25 per cent of the sample did not know the names of any of the first four books of the

New Testament (Matthew, Mark, Luke and John), in 1999 the figure was 43 per cent; while of those identifying themselves as 'Christians' 44 per cent did not know the names of all four Gospels. More remarkably, particularly given the public discussion of the issue, only 29 per cent of self-styled 'Christians' knew that the millennium marked the birth of Christ (63 per cent thought it celebrated 'something else').

Moreover, there is a further reason to look with some suspicion on revelations of significant trends in matters of fundamental importance. Intellectuals and social commentators have a tendency to exaggerate the significance of the times in which they live. No doubt this is due in part to the wish to have something notable to say to their contemporaries. A more profound motivation, perhaps, is a way of thinking that sees the course of events as a series of movements from one state or condition to another, and which finds reason to suppose that these movements must be dramatic. Even if the periods of transition are infrequent, the assumption that they occur, combined with the tendency to exaggerate the importance of the present, is enough to explain the sense of current drama.

Expressions of these styles of thought are everywhere to be seen: in the quality press, on radio and television, in current affairs and policy periodicals, and so on, through to academic studies of this or that aspect of human life – or indeed of the life of the planet, the galaxy, and the cosmos. Thus, it is now said that we are witnessing the collapse of high civilisation; living at the end of art, politics and history; entering the age of post-sexual reproduction; setting a course for catastrophic depopulation; initiating a process of irreversible globalisation; facing unparalleled environmental disaster; possibly bringing about the conditions for the collapse of the universe through high-energy physics experiments; entering a disease-free era; inaugurating an age of agelessness, and so on. At a meeting of party leaders held in Malmo in 1997, the then newly-elected 'New Labour' British Prime Minister, Tony Blair, spoke of the 'veritable revolution of change' the world has been undergoing, and summarised his message by saying: 'New, new, new, everything is new.'

Three features of this way of thinking are worth noting. First, the tendency to 'presentism', as I shall call it, has been around for as long as people have tried to fashion accounts of the human condition and of the cosmos. It is not only in the 20th century that writers seemed to see signs of momentous change in their lifetimes. Philosophers from Plato to Marx have believed that their period was one of significant transformation, as have historians, artists, scientists, religious thinkers and others preoccupied with their place in the general scheme of things. Second, presentist claims are hard to contest. Assertions to the effect that we are living through the end of one thing or the beginning of another are usually difficult to assess, and when a pronouncement of decline or ascent is challenged the presentist always has a fall-back: claiming that the times are significant because they are ones of unparalleled stability or stasis. Third, while I included religious thinkers among those given to presentism, it would perhaps be more appropriate to say that the presentist tendency is itself a quasi-religious one in as much as it aspires to find transcendent significance in mundane events, and to prophesy apocalypse or salvation. This last point is deeply ironic in view of the assessment that religion is in a process of precipitous and irrecoverable decline. And the next most common view among Western intellectuals is that while we may not be at the end of religion we are certainly living through a period of unparalleled change in religious thought and practice.

Given the general suspicion of claims to the effect that present features are especially significant, and the difficulty of assessing such evidence as is presented, I am inclined to refrain from grand claims about extraordinary contemporary decline, ascent or unusual plateau-like continuity. So far as I am able to judge, the current condition of human affairs in general does not seem to be historically exceptional. Like the surface of the globe the course of events goes up and down, changing from one condition to another sometimes imperceptibly, sometimes dramatically; but just as no place is, as such, significant for being 'here' (the place one is located), so no time is, as such, significant for being 'now' (the period one is in). That is not to say that there are not significant forces at work or that our times might not be interesting. Indeed in a later chapter I shall be examining the whole idea of 'meta-narratives', including historical and religious ones. The present point, however, is just that whether one thinks of significant forces operating in the world as being human or divine, the same forces or analogous ones seem to have been at work in all periods of recorded history, and I cannot think of any period in which it could not have been said that they were 'interesting times'.

The writers of those texts classified by scholars as mythopoeic – Genesis and Exodus, the Epic of Gilgamesh, the Vedas and other ancient writings – report wars and strife, famines, diseases, floods, astronomical events and other blights and sights in terms that invested them with special significance. The patriarchs and prophets of Israel, Jesus and the early Christians, and Mohammed and his followers, all regarded their times as profoundly significant as periods of descent, ascent or transformation. So it was, is, and probably always will be. On that account I judge that the human situation now is pretty much the same as ever. As before, however, this is not to suggest that there are no large issues to be considered or that a religious interpretation in particular might not illuminate aspects of the contemporary world. The point, though, is that what it has to teach will be lessons also true of other times and places.

Consider in this connection the religious messages reported by the visionaries of Fatima in Portugal, once again made newsworthy by the decision of the Vatican in 2000 to reveal the text of the much speculated about 'Third Secret'. The background to this is as follows. Between 13 May and 13 October 1917, three young illiterate children, aged 10, 9 and 7, experienced a series of apparitions of a young woman who eventually identified herself as 'Our Lady of the Rosary' – in other words, the Mother of Jesus Christ (in the Orthodox churches the *theotokos*, the mother of God). Mary told the 'seers' that she had been sent by her son with a message for the world. Coming in a period of intense and bloody warfare, these apparitions, and especially the widely attested 'miraculous' event of the dancing sun accompanying the last of them, attracted great attention, and there was enormous interest in what the Virgin had to say. Some of this was reported at the time and consisted in requests for prayer, contrition and reparation. Mary is said to have explained that war is a punishment for sin, and promised that peace would come if what she asked for on behalf of her Son were done. On the other hand, if mankind failed to turn back to God and persisted in defiance of his commandments, then war, disorder and famine could be expected. It was also prophesied that if what she had asked for were not accomplished, then Russia would spread its errors of atheism and materialism throughout the world, raising up wars and persecutions against the Church.

In all of the apparitions the Lady emphasised the necessity of prayer and acts of reparation and sacrifice. On 17 July she gave the children what has come to be known as the 'Secret'. This consisted of three elements, two of which were subsequently reported to the religious authorities and later made public. The first part concerned a vision of Hell 'where the souls of poor sinners go' and included a plea for prayers and sacrifices done for the sake of saving souls. The second part pro-phesied further wars in which millions would die. It also included a plea that the Pope and all the world's bishops collectively should consecrate Russia to her name, promising that if this were done disaster would be averted and Russia returned to Christianity.

The last part, the 'Third Secret', remained undisclosed until the Vatican's partial revelation on the occasion of the beatification of two of the children in May 2000. The formal Church acknowledgement of their 'blessedness' was conducted by John Paul II 19 years to the day after his attempted assassination by a Turkish terrorist in St Peter's, and on the 83rd anniversary of the first appari-tion. After recovering from the nearly fatal 1981 shooting, the Pope went to Fatima to pray at the site of the appearances. He also had the would-be-assassin's bullet welded into the crown of the statue of the Virgin at the shrine (and a second bullet placed by an image of the Virgin Mary at Jasna Góra in Poland). It was already clear by that point that the Pope believed that the Lady of the Rosary had interceded to save his life. But was that just a matter of personal piety perhaps supported by the coincidence of dates, or had he any other reason to think that there was a connection between the apparitions, the assassination attempt, and his survival of it?

Until May 2000 speculation about the Third Secret (a written version of which had been in the possession of the Vatican since April 1957) centred on two theories, both of which gathered support from the Vatican's refusal to reveal its contents. The first was that it continued the apocalyptic style of the earlier parts, prophesying a nuclear holocaust resulting from Russia's efforts at world domination. Advocates of this interpretation suggested that the details were too horrific to be announced, and even that doing so might lead the US to a pre-emptive first strike, thereby triggering a nuclear war. The second theory speculated that the message concerned corruption within the Church, indeed within the Vatican: not financial and sexual scandal but spiritual corruption – and perhaps even satanic possession. If that were so, if the very barque of Peter was not only being lashed by storms without but was under the control of inner forces that sought to sink it, then it was hardly likely that those very forces would reveal to the world a prophecy of their takeover.

The second view has been particularly popular among conspiracy theorists. Some are ultra-conservative Catholics opposed to Vatican II and unhappy about the Roman Church's efforts to come to terms with aspects of modern culture. Others link their interpretations of the Secret with various international conspiracies. The latter include a Masonic-Jewish pact designed to subvert true Christianity, a Communist-United Nations alliance aimed at instituting a world government of atheistic humanism, and a UFO-denial conspiracy in which the Western industrial-military complex is attempting to suppress the fact that extra-terrestrials are among us. By this last account the Lady of the Fatima apparition, and the 'Angel of

Peace' that is reported to have preceded her, were aliens come to communicate a message to earthlings. Such are the fantasies into which some religious imaginations drift.

A clue to the truth was already available in John Paul II's early public visit to Fatima after the assassination attempt, and in the less well known fact that when he recovered consciousness after the shooting he asked for the file containing the Fatima text and read the Secret. The crowds assembled in May 2000 for the beatification ceremony were the first outside a small circle of Popes and senior officials to be told of its content. To general amazement at the end of the Mass, and with Papal approval, the Vatican Secretary of State, Cardinal Sodano, announced that the Secret indeed related to a prophetic vision concerning 'above all the war waged by atheistic systems against the Church and Christians, and it describes the immense suffering endured by witnesses to the faith in the last century of the second millennium'. The vision showed a 'bishop, clothed in white [the traditional Papal colour]. As he makes his way with great difficulty towards the Cross amid the corpses of those who were martyred (bishops, priests, men and women religious and many laypeople), he too falls to the ground, apparently dead, under a hail of gunfire.' According to the remaining visionary, Lucia dos Santos, who is a nun in an enclosed Carmelite Convent in Coimbra, but who met the Pope at Fatima, the children had taken the figure to be a pope. So too, it seems, had John Paul II, who is quoted as saying that a 'mother's hand guided the bullet's path' so that he might 'halt at the threshold of death'. (One of his widely-published works is entitled *On the Threshold of Hope*.)

What is to be made of all of this? It certainly has features commonly associated with religious super-naturalism: apparitions, wondrous sights in the sky, apocalyptic visions, prophesies, miraculous interventions, and secrets conveyed from Heaven to Earth. In these respects it conforms to a common idea of medieval Christianity, with its mystic seers, miracles, shrines and pilgrimages. For many, now as then, that is its appeal; but for others concerned with 'reasonable religion', it is evidence of a tendency towards superstition. This is a frequently-voiced charge, but it is not clear that it is warranted. Superstition involves hopes and fears directed towards fate and autonomous preternatural forces – i.e. independent powers. By way of illustration, consider two front-page reports from US weekly tabloids. The first followed the 11 September attacks on the World Trade Center and showed what it claimed was the sneering face of Satan in the black clouds billowing from the Twin Towers. The second report came in the weeks following the meeting between the Pope and American cardinals convened to discuss the priestly vice and abuse scandal. Again, the story drew in the demonic, now managing to link it with the Fatima Third Secret. According to the report, the main reason for the Vatican meeting was not to discuss the US scandal but to inform the Church leaders of the final part of the Fatima secret. As revealed 'exclusively' to the tabloid by a mystic source, this concerns the existence of an Antichrist 'Legion' who or which will soon launch the final attack of the forces of darkness in their effort to rule the world in the name of Satan.

Like similar stories of dark forces whose presence is known to visionaries and to readers of the signs, these appeal to the imagination, but though they involve religious imagery they are not as such sacred or theological narratives. The images are no more than surface attachments to tales of horror and superstition, no different in kind from folk-stories of evil mountains and ancient curses. Christianity, by contrast, involves belief in purposeful, almighty and benign divine governance. Nothing in the mere ideas of the visionary or of the miraculous is at odds with this latter religious conception but, equally, nothing in those ideas is itself properly religious.

It is also worth noting that if there is a tendency to superstition in the original Fatima story it is a common and unsurprising feature of popular religion in most cultures and at most times. With suitable modifications much of the same story could have been a Muslim tale, or again with appropriate adaptation a Hindu or Buddhist one. It is unlikely, I think, that modernising Christians who voice loud distaste for the business of Fatima would be so willing to denounce comparable miraculous narratives from other faiths. That, however, is surely not because they are more disposed to believe them to be true, but because they think that cultural respect is owing to others. What I cannot see is why the same respect is not owing to one's co-religionists.

It is interesting in this connection to consider the remarks of Bishop Spong concerning African Christians who at the Anglican Lambeth conference voiced traditional Church teachings on matters of sexuality. 'They had moved out of animism,' he said, 'into a very superstitious kind of Christianity. They have yet to face the intellectual revolution of Copernicus and Einstein that we have faced in the developing world; that is just not on their radar screen.' I shall explore something of the supposed significance for religion of the scientific revolution. For now, however, I am interested in what such remarks, and similar observations by religious critics of events such as those of Fatima, indicate about the critic's own outlook.

Perhaps they expect better of people whom they suppose to have the one true faith. This is an interesting thought, which features in the Torah ('Law') in the Hebrew Bible. It arises from God's selection of Abraham and his descendants to be his chosen people. To them great privileges would be given and from them, in return, great fidelity would be expected. The contract is implicit in the following promise of Yahweh to Moses: 'I am the Lord. I appeared to Abraham, to Isaac, and to Jacob, as God Almighty [*El Shaddai*], but by my name "the LORD" [*YHWH – Yahweh*] I did not make myself known to them. I also established my covenant with them ... Say therefore to the people of

Israel ... *I will take you for my people, and I will be your God*' (Exodus 6:2-7). A similar theme reappears in Christian scripture where what is at issue is God's grace bestowed on those who have heard and have believed: 'Everyone to whom much is given, of him will much be required' (Luke 12:48). As these references indicate, however, the notion of the special responsibility of those possessed of the unique revelation of God is old and decidedly pre-pluralistic, and not the sort of idea that generally features in modernist and postmodernist reconstructions of Judaism and of Christianity.

Returning to the story of Fatima, what about the *content* of the Third Secret, as of the whole text of the message relayed by Lucia? Does it present something distinctly for the present age – a testament to times of unparalleled tribulation, or a new scheme of salvation? References to the shooting of a religious figure are in an obvious respect contemporary, though the general idea of priestly martyrdom goes back to the earliest Christian times and there is no shortage of non-Christian counterparts. It was not until 1944, nearly thirty years after the early deaths of her co-visionaries, that Sister Lucia wrote down the Third Secret, during a period when many feared that the life of a Pope might well end in a burst of gunfire. More interestingly, Cardinal Sodano was careful to avoid disappointment at a text which might seem less than precisely prophetic in the popular sense of being precognitional. He said that the vision's content had to be interpreted 'in a symbolic key' and that it did not 'describe photographically the details of future events, but synthesised and compressed, against a single background, facts which extend through time in an unspecified succession and duration', but also that it concerned 'the immense suffering endured by witnesses to the faith in the last century of the second millennium'.

It is now worth asking two questions: first, could this last concern equally well be related to those of other denominations and faiths; and, second, could an equivalent message have been equally aptly delivered in the 19th century, or earlier? I believe the answer to both questions is clearly 'yes'. Jews, most obviously, have endured immense suffering in witnessing to their faith; so too have Muslims, Hindus, Buddhists, Sikhs – and the list goes on. Similarly, such suffering has featured for as long as religious history has been recorded. In short, the message of Fatima gives particular and local expression to a general truth about the human condition: it is often conflicted, cruel and violent, and the just and the holy can expect to be persecuted.

My point is not to attack or defend the veracity of the reported visions, but only to point out that when one abstracts from the contextual detail of such mystical deliverances, the message tends to be apt for all times and places. This is not to say that it is trivial or unlikely to have a transcendent source. On the contrary, it would be odd to think that a religious message for humankind would be merely for some here and some now rather than for all times and places. Presentism is not only philosophically doubtful; it is also religiously suspect and spiritually shallow.

As I have said, however, it does not follow that attention to historical events and trends cannot be illuminating, or even that opinion polls might not have something to tell us about the state of a nation. What the surveys I began with inform us about is not a nation's 'soul', but its familiarity with and comprehension of religious ideas and teachings – more a matter of its intellectual than its spiritual condition. In this respect, at least, there is an incontestable truth in the secularist thesis: namely that in contemporary Western societies, and increasingly in other parts of the world to which those societies have exported their popular culture, there is growing ignorance of things religious. For secular humanists and scientific atheists that is as it should be. For committed believers it is a matter for profound sadness. Whose attitude is the right one cannot be determined by consulting polls past, present or future, but only by considering the coherence, plausibility and truth of fundamental religious claims. The most important question that an intelligent person can pursue in considering the issue of religion is not whether people believe in it, but whether they should.

2

Religion, Science and
the Universe

Even the bad achievements of science work.
The achievements of theologians don't do anything.
Richard Dawkins

Since the publication of *The Selfish Gene* (1976), Richard
Dawkins has become an increasingly prominent figure in
debates about the nature and value of scientific enquiry,
particularly in relation to human origins, and about the
relationship between science and religion. Indeed A.N.
Wilson recently described him as 'Darwin's most ardent
representative on Earth' (the reference being to the traditional characterisation of the Pope as 'God's representative
on Earth'). Over the same period Dawkins has written a
number of other successful presentations of evolutionary
ideas. By his own lights, and by those of many others, he
is a spokesman on behalf of unprejudiced reason and
sound understanding. According to another perspective,
however, Dawkins represents the arrogance and intellectual imperialism of a worldview that would reduce all
reality to aggregates of particles or packages of energy.

Not unreasonably, Dawkins rejects this latter characterisation of his position, denying that in his scientific view human beings are 'nothing but' collections of particles. On the contrary, he believes them to be incredibly complex, multi-part functioning systems with properties we barely begin to understand. Nonetheless, in common with many others, Dawkins does believe that we are material beings in a wholly material universe. Accordingly, in some manner which we may not yet understand, everything that is true of us – our biochemistry, our physiology, our sentience and intellectual powers and even our longings for salvation and immortality – is the product of millions of years of increasingly complex physical interactions. Additionally, the very existence of the material out of which the universe is composed and the causal laws that govern the behaviour of that matter are themselves facts of nature, neither calling for nor being made any more intelligible by appeal to a supernatural creator. This is evidently an economical view; whether it is an explanatorily adequate one remains to be seen.

Without for the moment pursuing the question of reductionism it would be fair to describe Dawkins and those who share his view as 'scientific naturalists'. This outlook involves more than simply a belief in the objectivity and value of science: it is a philosophical worldview. Scientific naturalists believe that all reality is natural (no non-physical beings, no miracles, no vitalist or mentalist forces), and that the proper method of describing and explaining nature is empirical science.

Evidently, such a stance excludes religion other than as a social phenomenon. And, as the quotation opening this chapter suggests, it is unlikely that Dawkins believes that an independent audit will find religion to have been of much benefit. It will recognise that some have done good to others from religious motives; but the point may be made that the value of such behaviour can be established on a non-religious basis. How else indeed could the independent auditor weigh the good deeds of religious believers unless they were recognisable as good independently of their presumed religious motivation?

The issue of religion and morality is a theme to which I shall return. Here, though, I am concerned with the basic opposition between scientific naturalism and theism as to whether the existence and character of the universe is naturalistically explicable, or whether only the hypothesis of a creator God can account for it. So far as the second suggestion is concerned, it is necessary first to point out that the centuries have produced a highly significant change in the way in which many, if not most, theologians and religiously-inclined philosophers think about the project of proving God's existence from the fact and structure of the natural order.

The heyday of such speculation was the Middle Ages, when metaphysicians of each of the 'religions of the book' developed the field of *natural theology*. Three of the greatest figures were the Muslim Avicenna (Ibn Sina); the Jew Maimonides (Moshe ben Maimon) and the Christian Aquinas (Tommaso d'Aquino). The first lived in Persia from 980 to 1037; the second in Islamic Spain and then in Egypt from 1135 to 1204; and the third was born and died in Italy (*c.* 1225 and 1274 respectively), though he travelled widely and taught in Paris, as well as in Rome and Naples. Such were the intellectual affinities between these figures, with Aquinas openly and respectfully drawing upon Avicenna and Maimonides, that they are occasionally depicted together in later medieval paintings. One of the best examples can be seen in the Spanish Chapel of Santa Maria Novella in Florence. Ranks of seated figures lead the eye upwards to a Gothic throne around which angels hover. Placed serenely at the centre of attention is the figure of Aquinas. On his lap rests his great work, the *Summa Theologiae*, held open to face the viewer; and there at his feet – though not looking up to him – are the figures of his Jewish and Islamic predecessors.

Drawing on the philosophies of Plato and Aristotle, these and other metaphysicians of the period developed an understanding of knowledge which they characterised as 'science' (*scientia*). This involved the notion of a complete system of propositions ordered by their logical relations, with first principles at the top and statements concerning detailed phenomena at the bottom. It was a matter of much debate how exactly the first principles of science might be discovered, but once they had been arrived at other claims would then be logically deducible from them. This way of thinking involves a very demanding account of what an adequate argument should be like. Technically speaking it must be a 'demonstration':

that is, it must start with premises that are beyond doubt; and it must proceed by deduction, thereby arriving at indubitable conclusions. Thus, when in the *Summa Theologiae* Aquinas asks 'whether it can be demonstrated that God exists', he is asking whether God's existence can be known *for certain* by deducing it from other indubitable facts. Scientific explanations often infer effects from the nature of their causes, as when an explosion is explained by reference to the properties of certain materials. In the case of Aquinas's proofs, however, the demonstration proceeds in the opposite direction: from effect to cause and more precisely *from* what is observable in nature *to* its unobservable transcendent creative source.

Before discussing Aquinas's proofs I need to complete the contrast concerning changed attitudes to reasoning about the existence of God. While there is renewed interest in natural theology, most philosophers who favour theism are now inclined to think that there simply cannot be a strict *demonstration* of the existence of God, but only a probabilistic proof. In other words, an argument to the effect that given the world *it is more likely than not* that there is a God, or that God's existence *provides the best explanation* of things we observe. These lesser claims may seem creditably modest when compared with old-style natural theology. However, they may also be seen as consequences of an increasing scepticism about the powers of the human mind to establish, with certainty, anything whatsoever. Moreover, the idea that the existence of God is a probable fact leaves one wondering how, if other explanations are deemed possible, it can be anything other than a conjecture. As such it must remain vulnerable as other theories are developed, or as the hope of them is clung to tenaciously by those committed to a Godless worldview. It is hard to see how a probabilist outlook could provide a philosophical framework for doctrinal theology, or the ground for self-sacrifice. A belief that is hostage to inconclusive evidence of the most general sort is unfitted to the role of providing such a framework or ground. Conjectures rarely call forth martyrs. Equally, though, even solid metaphysical bones do not by themselves make for a living faith.

There is a further and much greater difference between medieval and modern views, by comparison with which debates about probability as against certainty may seem largely irrelevant. For while pretty much everyone in the medieval world believed that nature pointed unmistakably to its divine authorship, the very idea of theism has come under increasing attack since the 18th century. So that today, among those who still consider such matters, the default position may well be agnosticism if not atheism. The charges against theism tend to be of three kinds. First, that it is incompatible with the existence of natural evils such as disaster, disease, deformity and pain. Second, that it was a primitive attempt to account for what could not properly be explained, long since made redundant by the advance of science. Third, that religious belief and practice has been shown by psychology and social science to have roots in primitive fears and appetites.

The first charge is an old one. It is classically presented in one of the most corrosive works of anti-theistic Enlightenment philosophy, *Dialogues Concerning Natural Religion* (1779) by David Hume (1711-76). I say 'anti-theistic' rather than 'atheistic' philosophy, since although he is often spoken of as an atheist, Hume's true position is hard to determine. In the *Dialogues*, one character, Philo, speaks as follows: 'Is the deity willing to prevent evil, but not able? then is he impotent. Is he able, but not willing? then is he malevolent. Is he both able and willing? whence then is evil?' Philo actually refers to the antiquity of the issue, describing these as 'Epicurus' old questions'. Epicurus lived between 342 and 270 BC, and there is a text from Lactantius from some six hundred years later which quotes him in similar terms. As interesting as the antiquity of the challenge, however, is the fact that it is one posed by religious believers to themselves.

Jews, more than any other theists, have had reason to ponder the reconcilability of evil with the existence of a good God – one who promised that they would be his people for whom he would care. Long before the Shoah, the Jews suffered greatly and produced ever more profound spirituality. The tradition began early: no one can read the Book of Job (especially chapters 38-42) with any degree of comprehension and not be struck by the thought that the 'problem of evil' is continuously to the fore, and yet, even though no intellectually satisfactory solution is provided, faith remains the dominant key.

Similarly, the inscrutability of God's ways is acknowledged unapologetically by St Paul in his Epistle to the Romans (11:33-34), where he quotes Isaiah (40:13): 'Who has directed the Spirit of the Lord, or as his counsellor has instructed him?' Answer: no one in their right minds.

These constitute spiritual reflections; but there are also theoretical treatments of the problem among premodernist philosopher-theologians. In the *Confessions*, written *c*. 397, St Augustine sets out the problem in a form close to that of Epicurus and Hume, and Aquinas makes the question of the compatibility of evil with the existence of a good God the subject of the article following the one in which he argues that God's existence may be demonstrated. The theoretical response to the challenge of evil is formally valid but few could suppose that it is religiously satisfying. It consists in effect in a 'contraposition' of the original challenge. The problem of evil can be expressed by saying 'if there is any unnecessary evil in the world then there is no God'. The theist responds by pointing out that this is logically equivalent to the claim 'if there is a God then there is no unnecessary evil in the world'. Affirming that there is a God the theist concludes that there is no *unnecessary* evil. In short, the problem of evil cannot usefully be considered independently of the positive case for atheism, most relevantly, the suggestion that there is evil that can have no justification or exculpatory explanation. I shall consider this in chapter 4.

For now we return to the question of whether observation and reason provide an argument for the existence of God. For most of the last two thousand years philosophy and religion have co-existed fairly happily together. To consider only the Western tradition: most of its greatest philosophers have also been theologically (as well as scientifically) minded. In addition to those already mentioned the list includes the following: Anselm of Canterbury (1033-1109), Bonaventure (1217-74), Descartes (1596-1650), Spinoza (1632-77), Locke (1632-1704), Leibniz (1646-1716), Berkeley (1685-1753), Reid (1710-96), Kant (1724-1804), Hegel (1770-1831), Kierkegaard (1813-55), William James (1842-1910), and Henri Bergson (1859-1941). Yet, as was noted, today only a small minority of leading philosophers believe in God. I want to say more about why that is so before trying to assess whether the current situation indicates that faith in a creator God is contrary to reason.

One might suppose that the reason why belief was previously more widespread among philosophers is a general cultural one, that in the past people as a whole were more disposed to belief than they are today. Philosophers share the general outlook of their times, so it is to be expected that in more religious times more of them will have been religious. Setting aside the question of whether philosophers do in fact share the beliefs of their cultures and times, this account is somewhat regressive: it invites the further question of why in the past people in general were more disposed to religious belief than is the case today. If things are indeed now different, why is this so?

The change is due principally to two different factors. First, to growing material affluence, which has shifted consciousness away from questions about the objective meaning and value of life towards choices about which tangible goods to acquire and which lifestyles to culti-vate. While the former tend to lead the mind towards Heaven, the latter tend to confine it to Earth. The second factor is the impact of natural science and associated ways of thinking. I shall consider questions of life's meaning and value later. With regard to the influence of science, while I disagree with his conclusions about the credibility of traditional religious ideas and the poss-ibility of their being given philosophical support, I think A.N. Wilson expresses very well the sense of doubt and even terror that overcame the educated classes in consequence of the naturalising project of 18th- and 19th-century scientific thought. Discussing the geologist Charles Lyell in *God's Funeral* (1999), Wilson writes: 'Lyell could show that God, if existent, could not possibly have brought the world into being, in all of its present geological formations, in six days. Darwin could make the even more disturbing discovery that Hume was right, and there was no need to posit a notion of purpose behind nature at all.'

These were indeed common conclusions among scien-tific men. The first is of lesser significance since even in the early centuries of Christianity it was recognised by

Augustine and others that the Genesis creation story should not be read literally, and by the Middle Ages that thought was common to Christian, Jewish and Islamic thinkers. But the idea that nature might not need a designer was and remains a threat to intelligent religious belief. It also contrasts sharply with the thought of the pre-Enlightenment periods. About twenty years after the crucifixion of Christ, St Paul wrote his Letter to the Romans, in which we read: 'What can be known about God is plain to men for God has shown it to them. Ever since the creation of the world his invisible nature, namely his eternal power and deity, has been clearly perceived in the things that have been made.'

This is sometimes cited as an early case of Christian philosophical theology. Paul, though, had little sympathy for metaphysics and belittled the 'wisdom of the Greeks'. His experience of philosophers was not a happy one. In Athens, having spoken in the public square about the 'resurrection', he was invited by Epicurean and Stoic teachers to set out the new teaching before the city council. Their interest may have rested on a confusion, for in Greek the feminine noun for 'resurrection' (*ana-stasis*) could be taken for the name of a goddess. At any rate when they heard about Jesus being crucified and rising from the dead the general reaction seems to have been ridicule (Acts 17:32), and when he writes to the church he founded in Corinth, Paul is fairly scathing about 'the wise', the scholars' and 'the skilful debaters of this world', adding: 'we proclaim the crucified Christ, a message that is offensive to the Jews and nonsense to the Gentiles' (1 Corinthians 23). In the Romans passage, therefore, Paul is not so much offering a philosophical proof as reminding his readers that the world is the product of a creator. However, reasoning from the wonders of nature to the existence of God was common in antiquity and would have been known to Paul and to the educated Roman Jews and converts to whom he was writing. For example, in his dialogue *On the Nature of the Gods* (*De natura deorum*), composed around 45 BC but set some thirty years earlier, Cicero has the Stoic philosopher Quintus Lucillus Balbus say: 'The point hardly needs affirming. What can be so obvious and clear, as we gaze up at the sky and observe the heavenly bodies, as that there is some divine power of surpassing intelligence by which they are ordered?'

In the centuries that followed, Jewish, Christian and Islamic thinkers aimed to start with facts evident to any thoughtful person and to show that these imply the existence of a creator. As was said, the most famous presentation of such arguments is to be found in Aquinas's *Summa Theologiae*. There Thomas sets out the five ways (*quinque viae*) of proving the existence of God. While many educated people recognise the phrase 'the five ways', too few have actually read the text. This is probably because it is assumed that the proofs are forbiddingly difficult to understand or that they are expressed at great length and in strange language. In fact, however, the arguments are presented in the course of a couple of pages, and in a modern translation such as that provided by Timothy McDermott, which glosses technical terms, they are not very hard to comprehend (see his excellent *Selected Philosophical Writings of Thomas Aquinas*). Here, for example, are extracts from Aquinas's first and fifth ways (with slight adjustments to the McDermott translation):

The first and most obvious way is the argument from change. It is evident from experience, and quite certain, that some things are in process of change [e.g. in respect of location, speed, size, temperature and so on]. Now whatever is changing is being changed by something else … and if this other thing is itself in process of change then it is being changed by yet another thing; and that thing in turn by another. But this cannot go on forever or else there will be no first cause and, in consequence, no subsequent causes of change … Thus we arrive at some first cause of change which is not itself being changed by anything, and this is what everyone understands by *God* …

The fifth way is based on the governance of nature. We observe that things in nature act for a purpose which is apparent from their acting generally in the same ways and for the sake of some good. [For example, flowers turn towards the light, birds make nests, hearts circulate blood, etc.] But whatever lacks awareness cannot act for the sake of an end except by being directed towards it by one who does have knowledge and intelligence, just as the arrow is directed by the archer towards its [i.e. the archer's] target. Therefore everything in nature is directed to its goal by one with knowledge and intelligence, and this we call *God*.

Very broadly speaking, arguments from the world to God come in two forms corresponding to Aquinas's several proofs. First, those that reason from the existence of something that might not have been or which is not self-explanatory, to the existence of something that is *necessary* – these are grouped under the heading *cosmological arguments*. Second, those arguments that reason from the orderly character of things to the existence of a *designer*. These are classified as *teleological arguments*. Arguments of both sorts originate in antiquity and became popular in the Middle Ages, when they were carefully developed and refined. They continued to be favoured by philosophers until the 18th century. Thereafter, however, they came to be questioned and today they are highly contested.

There are several reasons for this decline in standing. One I have mentioned already, namely the fact that in the medieval and early modern periods they were very ambitiously presented as arguments whose premises were entirely evident and hence beyond doubt, and in which the inference to the conclusion that God exists was unquestionable. The general effect of scepticism has been to cause philosophers and others to dispute whether *any* statement whatsoever is beyond doubt or contention. Also, it has come to be held that there could be other explanations of the phenomena cited and hence the very most that could be said is that these phenomena are more likely to have been produced by God than to have arisen naturally. Though whether we really know what these explanations might be is a further matter.

Consider standard forms of (a) *cosmological* and (b) *teleological* arguments:

a) 1. Some things change.
   2. If any things change then there must be an uncaused cause of change.
   3. Therefore there is an uncaused cause of change.

b) 1. Some things exhibit regularity.
   2. If any things exhibit regularity then there must be an uncreated designer.
   3. Therefore there is an uncreated designer.

It might be thought that the first premise in each argument is indeed beyond dispute, but that assumption fails to take account of the ingenuity of scepticism and other philosophical querying of the apparently evident. More significantly the second premise in each case is nowadays quite widely challenged. It is here, I suggest, that the influence of scientific as well as philosophical thought shows itself. Consider in particular the second argument, which has seemed most vulnerable to the advance of scientific understanding. Whereas it was once thought to be the case that the regularity of the tides, seasons, planetary motions, and so on, and the existence and operation of organs that benefit the animals that possess them, could only be explained by reference to an extra-natural source of order, these assumptions are now taken to be disproved by theoretical physics and neo-Darwinian evolutionary theory. This is not the occasion to pursue these matters in great detail, but let me offer a couple of comments in support of the traditional theological proofs.

The regularity of nature from the macroscopic to the microscopic levels is well-attested. Even the mysterious quantum phenomena exhibit significant statistical patterns. Although it may not be determinate when a particle will be emitted, the fact is that this remains within a range of probability that renders the phenomena systematic. So, whether we are dealing with determinate or probabilistic propensities we still find nature to be orderly, and this fact is not self-explanatory. It may be said that if it were not orderly there would have been a cosmic collapse and we would not have existed to raise our questions. This hardly eliminates the wonder. Our existence allows the fact of natural order to be observed but had we not existed that order would still have been there; thus the issue of its origin is a real one. Either we look for an explanation of it, or we say in advance that there is none. Adopting the first option, it is hard to see what the conclusion could be, save that order results from the activity of a creator. Adopting the second involves a markedly unscientific assumption. It ill-suits the scientifically minded, therefore, to say that belief in a creator is incompatible with the scientific outlook.

The Darwinian challenge to natural theology is more limited in scope, in that it does not purport to offer a non-theological account of the universe as a whole. Yet it has been much more extensive in its effect. Indeed, it is largely with this in mind that Wilson remarks: 'It would be a bold philosopher in the late 20th century who thought he could prove the existence of God.' The evolutionary challenge need not reject the claim that there is regularity, but only question the suggestion that the complexity of organisms, the behaviour of living parts and wholes, and the adaptation of all of this to the natural environment calls for a divine explanation. Instead, it postulates random mutation among species groups, plus natural selection of certain populations in virtue of the adaptive utility of their mutant features given the current environments. Thus, if some populations sprout hair and this offers protection against heat or cold then, *ceteris paribus*, these animals are more likely to survive and breed, and this or related features among their descendent groups will again be selected for. On it goes, and by stages emerge highly adapted animals such as us. Wonderful to contemplate and not difficult to explain – at least in principle.

The idea that regularity or order in nature might be the product of blind chance had a devastating impact upon 19th-century theologians and intellectually sophisticated believers. Darwin gave up his own religious belief, notwithstanding that he concludes *The Origin of Species* with a reference to 'life … having been originally breathed by the Creator into a few forms or into one'. In the 19th century few intelligent and educated persons in the Anglo-Saxon Protestant world would have been familiar with the arguments of Aquinas's *Summa Theologiae*, though they might have heard of them in the manner of someone remotely acquainted with historical literature.

Such scholastic writings were generally ignored as belonging to the largely obscure, pre-scientific, priest- and monk-ridden Middle Ages. By contrast, however, the arguments of the Cambridge don and Anglican clergy- man William Paley (1743-1805) seemed modern, scientific and supportive of belief. Paley opens his work gravely entitled *Natural Theology; or Evidences of the Existence and Attributes of the Deity, Collected from the Appearances of Nature* with the following words:

> In crossing a heath, suppose I pitched my foot against a stone, and were asked how the stone came to be there, I might possibly answer, that for anything I knew to the contrary it had lain there forever; nor would it, perhaps, be very easy to show the absurdity of this answer. But suppose I had found a watch upon the ground, and it should be enquired how the watch happened to be in that place, I should hardly think of the [same] answer ... Yet why should this answer not serve for the watch as well as for the stone? For this reason, and for no other, namely, that when we come to inspect the watch, we perceive – what we could not discover in the stone – that its several parts are framed and put together for a purpose ... This mechanism being observed and under- stood, the inference we think is inevitable, that the watch must have had a maker.

Paley later identifies biological examples which he argues are analogous to mechanical systems such as the watch. He discusses, for example, the structure of the heart, its various interacting parts and their role in sustaining its function as a pump. Likewise the eye. He also considers animal behaviour including nest-building, arguing that these innate and unreflective tendencies constitute beneficial natural systems. The general point is clear enough. For Paley and for his appreciative readers it was evident that nature provides abundant examples of intelligent design. And since it was not supposed that these might be the work of super-aliens the conclusion could only be that the universe is the handiwork of God.

Since we are now familiar with the general form of evolutionary explanations, it is hard to imagine how immune to scepticism Paley's reasoning must have seemed. It was the genius of Darwin (and others) to conceive of how the same effects could have resulted from random mutation operating over multitudes of generations. The Darwinian story would have no plausibility if the Earth were as young as Biblical chronology suggested, but this is where the work of geologists such as James Hutton and Charles Lyell fitted into the naturalistic picture. In his *Principles of Geology* (1830-34), Lyell set out sound methods and results which showed the Earth to be millions of years old and to contain fossils of long extinct species (current estimates date some rocks to 3.8 billion years). It was Lyell who persuaded Darwin to publish his account of the origin of species and who even arranged for its publication.

The Paleyean case was undermined and so, by implication, were other arguments from order and regularity. It was previously judged inconceivable that the natural world could be anything other than the product of intelligent design – something that in his *Natural History of Religion* (1757) even Hume appeared to concede. Thanks to Darwin and others of the period, it then appeared that the conjunction of chance, circumstance and vast stretches of time was sufficient to account for the whole of nature. So it was, and largely still is assumed. But matters are more complex. When looked at in detail and from the perspective of a wide-ranging view of nature and the plurality of forms it contains, evolutionary explanations are far from compelling. Here I set aside the particular problems posed for Darwinian theory by the apparent non-incremental change suggested by the fossil record. What the record reveals are often accumulations of change whose rate was too slow to match known evolutionary developments. But these 'gaps' only challenge the account of evolution as always occurring by natural selection and do not necessarily undermine the general idea.

I am concerned instead with certain philosophical difficulties. First, there are features of human life whose adaptive utility is difficult to demonstrate. These include consciousness, and an aptitude for philosophy, theology and other abstract thought, including theoretical science. It is unclear how, for example, abilities to think about the nature of numbers, or to ponder the meaning of human suffering, or to evaluate the extent of our moral duties to non-human animals, or to comprehend the nature of space-time, confer any survival advantage on human groups or on the whole species. Yet these sorts of capacities seem to be precisely what mark us out as rational animals. So put, however, this thought might seem more of a challenge to the possible completeness of evolutionary explanation than to the very possibility of it accounting for material aspects of human nature.

Second and more generally problematic, however, is the fact that the very process of evolution seems to require non-evolved features. Let me point to two cases of the latter difficulty. First the problem of 'irreducible complexity'. This and related phrases feature prominently in an extended argument against Darwinian evolutionary theory recently presented by Michael Behe, an American professor of biochemistry. In *Darwin's Black Box: The Biochemical Challenge to Evolution* (1996), Behe begins with the point that Darwin had no idea of the underlying mechanism of evolution. That is, while he postulated random mutation leading to differential survival and breeding success, he did not know what the fundamental source and medium of change and transmission were. That itself is no criticism. The point, however, is that the subsequent understanding of the genetic basis of life and inheritance has lead to an appreciation of the peculiar complexity of the underlying biochemistry. It is not just that this is astonishingly intricate but that it involves systems which exhibit interdependent functionality in their parts.

One of Behe's favourite examples is the bacterial flagellum. This is an element embedded in the membrane of a cell which acts, in effect, as a rotary propeller. The 'motor' itself is located at the base of the flagellum and is made up of various parts. The intricate, microscopic detail is quite remarkable, though as Dawkins points out, intricacy and complexity are, as such, no bar to a natural-istic, non-design explanation. Behe's additional claim, however, is that this and other systems at the biochemical level which subserve the sort of species development that interested Darwin have the property that they can only function if all the parts are present and interacting. Thus one cannot suppose that the system developed in parts, first one bit and then another, or that it resulted from an accidental coming together of several elements. The whole thing only works if all the parts are in place and operating. By way of analogy Behe offers the example of a mousetrap. This is comprised of various components: base, spring, catch, etc., and if any one part is absent the thing is defunct. One cannot have a more primitive func-tioning version without a spring, or without a base, and so on. It is either all or nothing. For the same reason the bacterial flagellum's structure and operation cannot be explained as evolving from something more primitive that lacked either aspect.

It does not follow that if there are systems that exhibit this kind of irreducible complexity they must have come into being all at once and in an instant. After all, mouse-traps are just such systems, and nobody supposes that there is anything mysterious about their origins. But in this case we know how the thing is done: a designer conceives and composes the mechanism. The flagellum, however, is not a human artefact, and if such a thing were the product of extraterrestrial alien design and manufacture then that would just push the problem one stage back. Behe's conclusion is evident. The theory of evolution ultimately relies upon elements which could not themselves be products of natural evolution. These building blocks either exist mysteriously and without explanation, or they are explicable in the manner of the mousetrap – as products of design.

Here I have strengthened Behe's neo-Paleyean argument beyond the version which he himself presents. His position is that no plausible natural account of the origins of the bacterial flagellum – and similar irreducibly complex natural systems – has been advanced and that none seems likely to be forthcoming. But that makes his argument a case of inference to the best explanation, or perhaps into a probability argument. In other words it has the form: the best or most likely explanation of this sort of complexity is that it is the product of design rather than chance. So conceived it is still of interest, but as one who sympathises with the older medieval ambition to arrive at conclusive proofs I am inclined to treat it in the stronger way summarised as follows:

c) 1. Some things in nature exhibit irreducible systemic complexity.
    2. If any things in nature exhibit irreducible systemic complexity, then ultimately there must be an uncreated designer.
    3. Therefore there is an uncreated designer.

This argument can be blocked by denying either premise 1 or 2. Given what has already been said in support of 1, attention turns to 2. The price of rejecting it (while still accepting 1) is foregoing the possibility of any explanation of a phenomenon which is intrinsic and central to biology, and not just to its evolutionary aspect. This is not just unreasonable in the sense of being excessive, it is contrary to reason. Medieval scholars recognised that philosophical, scientific and every other kind of rational enquiry turns on the 'principle of sufficient reason'. Enquiry looks for an explanation and only comes to a conclusion in that which is self-explanatory. Certainly we may declare at some point that 'there is no explanation', meaning by this that we do not yet have one. To say, however, that there simply is *no* explanation is not to conclude an enquiry, it is to abandon one. Once we have started on the path in search of the origins of existence, of change, of regularity and of order, it is irrational, and *a fortiori* unscientific, to refuse to accept what emerges as the only available explanation, preferring to say that, after all, the matter might simply not be explicable.

Before concluding, let me state in brief a second argument against the adequacy and completeness of evolutionary theory as a general account of the origins of life – a longer presentation and defence of this is given in *Atheism and Theism* (1996 2nd edition, 2003), a debate between me and the philosopher J.J.C. Smart. Like Behe's, the argument concerns the biological sphere, but it differs in being focused on reproduction. Responding to the lack of adequate fossil evidence to support the thesis that the formation of new species is the result of accumulated mutation, some theorists have proposed the idea of 'punctuated equilibrium'. The late Stephen Jay Gould argued that evolutionary change may occur quite rapidly after long periods without significant development. Even so, no one supposes that one species simply evolves from another by a single step. Rather the idea is that there is 'cumulative selection': progressive sifting and sorting as survivors of one phase of selection are subjected to another environmental test. Evidently this supposes that there is already in place some form of reproduction possessed by the original and successor generations. Yet reproduction is an adaptive feature to be explained by selection no less than are others. But how can it be? Selection operates over generations, and successive generations only come into being through the replicative powers of their ancestors. These powers cannot themselves be the product of cumulative selection, and so their existence remains to be explained.

As in the strengthened version of Behe's argument, the conclusion must be that, there being no possible natural explanation of these facts, there is either no explanation at all, or there is a theistic one. But I have also argued that the 'no explanation' option is unsatisfactory to a rational enquirer. Where natural science can offer no explanation but theology can do so, then it is irrational to resist the latter; assuming its coherence, reason requires one to accept the theistic explanation. Nothing here is hostile to science. The point is only that while science may explain events and circumstances *within* a pre-existing natural framework, it is not equipped to explain the preconditions of the possibility of there being a natural order, or of its containing complex reproductive organisms. The implication is not that science should be rejected, but that the attempt to reject rational faith on the basis of a purported 'scientific worldview' is bogus.

In the face of the anti-religious triumphalism of Dawkins and the marginally lesser presumption of Wilson, I have argued that there is life in the old arguments for the existence of God. I have also indicated how believers may equip themselves to defend their faith on the basis of reasoning that has the power to elicit respect from the genuinely scientifically minded. If I am correct, then the achievement of philosophical theology in establishing the existence of God explains both why science can work, and why some of science's achievements are bad. The first because the world has an intelligible order to which science can conform itself; the second because there is also a moral order which the use of these scientific achievements may violate. Neither fact is something that science itself can explain. Yet both are explained on the assumption that the world is the product of intelligent design.

3

Religion and the Nature of Evil

Thro' many dangers, toils and snares, I have already
come, 'tis grace that brought me safe thus far,
And grace will lead me home.
John Newton

In the previous chapter I quoted Darwin's remark to the
effect that there is 'grandeur in the view of life … having
been originally breathed by the Creator into a few forms or
into one'. In all likelihood he was writing in terms conces-
sive to a position that he did not really hold. For the great
achievement of the theory of natural selection seemed to
lie precisely in its capacity to explain apparent order and
purpose in nature *without* having to trace them to an intelligent designer. Certainly in other private contexts Darwin
admitted to having given up religious belief. Even so, he
was right to note that evolution is not incompatible with
the idea of creation. The theory of common ancestry and
evolutionary descent imply that the enormous spread of
life-forms derives from a smaller initial base. In itself the
evolutionary hypothesis is silent on the issue of how life
originated; nor does it address the ultimate question of why
there is anything rather than nothing.

Many scientifically-minded theists focus on this last 'existential' point, resting their case for God on some version of the cosmological argument. While conceding that nothing about the structure and operations of the world resists naturalistic explanation, they insist that the fact that the universe exists at all is neither naturalistically explicable nor itself self-explanatory. Here one may recall the remark of Wittgenstein (1889-1952): 'It is not *how* things are in the world that is mystical, but that it exists' (*Tractatus Logico-Philosophicus*, 1922). Thus, they argue, the *being* of the world must be due to the work of an uncaused cause of being and of change: a divine creator. While sympathetic to cosmological arguments of this sort, I have tried to show how the order apparent in nature, and more precisely the very order that evolutionary theory claims to explain, is not accounted for by the theory itself. Indeed it cannot be, since evolutionary theory presumes the prior existence of both irreducible complexity and reproductive power in order to explain the very process of speciation by natural descent.

One possible response to this, not questioning the claim but seeking to cause embarrassment for its theistic conclusion, is suggested by a remark of A.N. Wilson at the outset of *God's Funeral*. He writes, with somewhat Humean irony, that:

> If you pressed the argument from Design too far you might infer a God who was curious about a multiplicity of life-forms, entirely unconcerned about the blood-

iness and painfulness with which so many of these forms sustained life while on this planet, a God who was no more demonstrably interested in the human race than he was in, say, beetles, of which he created an inordinately large variety.

I take the latter to be an allusion to the saying of the atheist scientist J.B.S. Haldane, who, when asked what nature had taught him about the creator and his creation, replied: 'God has an inordinate fondness for beetles.' Of course it is not only the varieties and numbers of beetles that are plentiful. Confining the inventory to Earth, there are multitudes of life-forms existing in conditions that are sometimes co-operative but are often competitive. These facts are taken to be a challenge to the special standing of humankind which is a common assumption of Judaism, Christianity and Islam, though less obviously a feature of Eastern religions. And they raise questions about the possible purposes and benign intent of the creator.

The Judaeo-Christian tradition is deeply humanistic in regarding men and women as being the high point of natural creation. Certainly, other beings have featured in the scriptural narratives and in reflections on them, but usually as servants of God (angels) or as servants of men (asses and oxen, etc.). In one respect, as spiritual beings, angels are closer to God. Famously, however, it is just such a non-human created person, namely Satan (formerly 'Lucifer'), who represents the worst of fallen creation, featuring both as a disloyal and vainglorious spirit and as a lowly animal. In the latter case, as a serpent in Paradise, he is also the corrupter of mankind. For this he is condemned: 'to crawl on your belly and to eat dust as long as you live' (Genesis 3:14). So far as scripture in general is concerned, animals are in the background. In the medieval world, travel and the development of scientific interests led to the compilation of bestiaries in which real, reported and imagined creatures of all sorts were drawn and described. It was not until the modern period, however, with the development of the microscope and the growth of natural history, that mankind really began to become aware of just how far the animal kingdom ranged beyond the population of the Ark.

Earlier I said that if the theist could show there is an all-good, all-knowing, all-powerful creator and sustainer of the universe, then he or she is in a position to counterpose the argument from evil so as to conclude that there is no unnecessary evil. In pursuing this strategy I also wish to provide a broader account of the nature and variety of evil as these appear from a religious perspective, and to suggest how the fact of evil might best be coped with. Note first the qualification 'unnecessary' evil. It will not be a refutation of the existence of a good God if evil is not something that even a wholly beneficent and omnipotent creator could have avoided, either because it is somehow a necessary concomitant of a good which it does not outweigh, or because it arises in some other way from creation, without itself being created. That is, the *philosophical* problem of evil is the problem of gratuitous, superfluous or totally overwhelming evil, evil that has no adequate justification or that outweighs the overall good of the world.

To say that there is no unnecessary evil, therefore, is neither to deny the reality of evil nor to diminish its significance. Yet that is precisely what some religious perspectives have done, and one may wonder whether this bolder strategy is not the better course. After all, the religious understanding claims to see meaning and value where the scientific view sees only matter and blind causality. Typically, religion also places that meaning within some transcendental narrative. What story could be better than that suffering and death are an illusion, and that quite generally, and notwithstanding appearances to the contrary, all is really good? In the *Dhammapada*, a collection of sayings ascribed to the Buddha and often memorised by his followers, we find this:

> All existing things are transient. One who knows and observes this ceases to be in the grip of grief.
> All existing things are caught up in suffering. One who knows and observes this ceases to be in the grip of grief.
> All existing things are unreal. One who knows and observes this ceases to be in the grip of grief.

Similar statements feature elsewhere in Buddhist writings and in other religious traditions that insist upon the un-reality of the world of appearances. The common response of these religions to the seeming facts of mortality and pain is to suggest that they are ultimately unreal. Hence, they are only of concern to those who are concerned by them and who are otherwise burdened by desire. The solution, then, is to cease to be troubled and to stop grasping at shadows. Knowing that things pass away, and accepting this without emotion, one will not then regard it as a cause for regret or anxiety. Through indifference, peace enters the soul. As the Buddha teaches: 'the cessation of suffering (*dunkha*) comes with absence of desire (*tanha*) and enlightened freedom (*nirvana*).'

There is certainly something to this. Anyone of even limited wisdom knows that much needless suffering is due to the attitudes and reactions of recipients of injury as much as to the cause of injury itself. How bad something is may depend upon how bad one lets it be. To that extent suffering is not beyond our control. We can lessen its impact by changing ourselves, by becoming less demanding of the world and of others, and more accepting of injury and loss. But as a general reply to the problem of evil, the Buddhist-style response faces two objections. First, unless one accepts the doctrines of *dharma* and in particular the belief in reincarnation, by which it may be held that all troubled and suffering creatures are somehow morally responsible for their condition, then the situation is that the cessation of suffering is only a possibility for those able to avail themselves of the teaching of a spiritual master. Dumb animals and dim humans will suffer *samsara* (endless wandering) without the possibility of self-applied meditative relief.

Whether this is unjust is not easily judged. 'It's not fair' is a common but often thoughtless refrain. Fairness is of proper concern where the distribution of burdens and benefits is at issue, but if there is no responsible distributor, just unknowing nature or a random procedure, then fairness is not in question. And if one's incapacity for redemptive meditation is due to one's own previous actions, then who is to blame? Still, even if injustice is not in question, it seems troubling to say that apparent evil is not a problem for those who can free themselves from it, but is one for those who cannot. Admittedly, there is in Buddhism the idea that those approaching enlightenment (*bodhisattvas*) may voluntarily forego their own escape from the wheel of birth, death and rebirth in order to be with the lowly, and to assist them in their own journey of ascent. These saintly figures are literally close to 'selflessness', having transcended the illusion of a persisting ego; and they are selfless too in the more familiar sense of putting others first. The question arises, though, of how they can help those who cannot help themselves. If it were simply a case of providing material comfort in the style of animal and human welfare volunteers, then we can see how they might do this. The problem, however, is that souls mired in base matter, and entangled in lowly troubles and terrors, have somehow to advance spiritually, and that can only be a movement from within.

It is usually said that the *bodhisattva* meditates for the sake of the unenlightened and that his sanctity can bestow blessings on others. This is reminiscent of the Christian idea of praying for one another, including, in the Catholic and Orthodox traditions, praying for the souls of the dead. Clearly there are parallels here, which have their counterparts in other religions; but there is also an important difference. In the Christian case there is a divine creator, sustainer, legislator, judge and executive. The 'economy of salvation' is managed by a providential deity, and so there is someone of infinite power, knowledge and goodness to whom to direct one's prayers – and to whom one can at least address the complaint 'it's just not fair'.

A principal (super)natural resource of that economy is *grace*, which is freely bestowed by God but may also be prayed for. In some Christian understandings, grace is provided universally, fully and inalienably; all receive it, cannot lose it and are thereby saved. In other accounts each person is provided with sufficient grace for salvation *if* they co-operate with it; but through their free choices they may diminish and ultimately extinguish the life of grace within their souls, and so render themselves incapable of being saved. Again, however, some Christians have held that grace is reserved to those whom God has chosen. This special elect cannot fail to be saved, but equally others cannot hope to earn grace no matter that they may proclaim Christian faith and do good works. Indeed, on this last grim view these seeming virtues are cruelly self-deluding, for without grace there is neither godliness nor goodliness. That it may seem otherwise only adds to the terrible drama, for no one really knows whether they are members of the elect or of the damned. The good may seem bad, and the bad good; for now, only God sees the truth, but in due course we will all know our place in the divine economy.

Apart from varying in their appeal, these different accounts of grace fit in with different ideas of creation. They are alike, though, in believing in divine governance, and so can find space for the idea that God might raise up lowly souls by infusing grace into them. He might do so in response to prayers of petition, or do so unbidden and for his own purposes. In any event we can give some definite content to the notion of imploring Heaven on behalf of those incapable of initiating their own upward movement. This idea engages a familiar religious hope captured in the image of the parent or spouse praying that God will reach into the soul of their child or partner and touch it with his grace. Many a woman has identified herself with Monica, the mother of St Augustine, who long petitioned on her son's behalf, happily living to see her prayers answered in his conversion. Without the idea of an all-powerful and loving God, it is hard to conceive how the sincere meditations of even the most selfless *bodhisattva* can move the souls of those who cannot move themselves. This is not to say that the saint's meditations will be inefficacious, only that if they play a part in the redemption of the lowly it will be because they have been taken note of by a deity of the sort which Buddhism does not itself recognise. It would be impossibly paradoxical for the non-theist to entertain this hope, but for the theist it should be taken as a mark of divine generosity that God does not restrict his beneficence to those who believe in him.

The second objection to Buddhist and related accounts of evil is that there is a tension between the claim that all existing things are caught up in suffering, and that all existing things are in some sense merely apparent and not real. If nothing is real then *a fortiori* there is no net of suffering. If there is no net of suffering then there can be no disentanglement from this, such as Buddhism promises. But if that promise is empty then so is the religion that defines itself in terms of it. So, if nothing is real, then Buddhism is null and void. Some may like the sound of the latter, as if it were itself a Zen verse (*koan*) setting a theme for meditation akin to the invitation to envisage the sound of one hand clapping. But if Buddhism has any chance of being true, then whatever it may mean to say that nothing is real this cannot be interpreted literally and without qualification.

A more restricted understanding of the idea of mere appearance is given in the suggestion that suffering itself is illusory. But if that is so then there is neither need nor scope for the *bodhisattva*'s therapy. Someone might reply that the doctrine of unreality concerns evil itself, and not the appearance or experience of it. As in other circumstances, we need to make a distinction between how things really are and how they seem. It may seem to the frightened child that there is a monster beneath the bed, but really there is nothing there. Reassurance takes the form of demonstrating that fact, and of getting the child to believe it. Likewise, might it not be that the truth about evil is that there is none, and may not the enlightened one resolve the problem by pointing this out? Here, though, the analogy lapses. While in the case of the child's fear the imagined monster is not a monster, in the case of the appearance of evil what are held to be near universal human illusions of pain and suffering are themselves evil. First, because they may themselves be painful and cause suffering. Second, because they represent a fundamental error about the nature of reality. Even if, as Buddhism teaches, pain is phenomenal, impermanent and without a definite essence, it is nevertheless real and a real evil. And to the extent that it *seems* other than as it is, there is then the further evil of human ignorance about matters of fundamental importance. I conclude, therefore, that things really are as we suppose: there is pain, suffering, ignorance, injustice and death, and these are indeed evils.

How then can the theist hope to sustain the case for God? If the world is God's creation and it contains evil, then is not God the author of this? To answer these questions it is necessary to observe the distinction between *moral evil*, which consists in intentional wrong-doing; and *natural evil*, which involves pain, loss, destruction and so on. The term 'moral' can here be understood narrowly as relating to specifically ethical responsibilities, or it may be taken broadly to refer to any kind of voluntary and intentional action in which values are at issue. In this second sense, someone who culpably creates ugliness or destroys beauty commits a moral evil, not because he has necessarily violated an ethical requirement but because he has certainly acted against an aesthetic one. Likewise, someone who knowingly promotes ignorance, or subverts the growth of knowledge, acts against the value of understanding, and so on for other kinds and spheres of values.

So far as moral evil in general is concerned, the solution lies in recognising that there is a great good in living a self-directed life. This, though, requires the capacity for judgment, deliberation and free action, and these are not trivial skills. Also, they can be used for bad as well as for good purposes. The sadistic teacher who takes pleasure in humiliating the most vulnerable child and who gives time to discerning the frailest spirit judges his victim 'well'. The terror bomber who calculates how to cause the greatest harm deliberates 'well'. The professional killer who isolates himself from every attachment and liberates himself from every compulsion and fear maximises his ability to act freely and to that extent acts 'well'.

In each case the favourable evaluation is not a moral one but concerns accuracy and effectiveness of procedure. Still, we can see that in creating the possibility of the good of deliberative free agency God also, and of necessity, allows the possibility of moral evil. One cannot create free beings while also constraining their actions so that they do only good, any more than in creating vision can one determine what the sighted will choose to look at. Indeed, were beings so constrained as to be able only to move towards the good, they would then not be authors of their actions but would be instruments of another agent. Accordingly, moral evil is not something that God creates, though it is something that he anticipates as a possible consequence of creating free agents. It is also something that he permits, and in some senses even co-operates with – he keeps the evil-doer in being, and sustains the food he eats, the air he breathes, the instruments he deploys and the victims he injures. Might one then say that in permitting evil the creator is morally culpable and hence cannot be a perfectly good God?

It is a familiar general principle, arising from the fact that an action typically has more than one effect, that while an agent is always morally responsible for what he *intends*, he may not be similarly responsible for what he foresees as resulting from his action. An example might be the surgeon who risks the death of his pregnant patient and that of her child as a consequence of a procedure aimed at saving the mother. This does not mean that in pursuing a good end it is permissible to tolerate any degree of collateral or consequential badness. There are some goods which it would otherwise be right to produce, even at the cost of some foreseen but unintended harm. But where the latter is disproportionate to the goods in question one must forego them, even at the cost of anti-cipated additional losses. A military commander, knowing that a group of terrorists bent on mass destruction is somewhere in a city, may perhaps risk some unintended deaths in his efforts to root out the would-be killers; but he may not secure the elimination of the threat they pose by simply annihilating the area of the city in which they are hiding, destroying both innocent and guilty alike. The general point is that an agent is not always and necessarily morally responsible for evils that may result from his (or another's) pursuit of the good, or from his (or another's) avoidance of other evils. Applying this to the case of the divinity the theist may claim first, that God does not create evil, though he may permit it; and, second, that such evil arises from the pursuit of a benign plan in which free agents are created with the intention, but without the compulsion, that they come to know, to love and to serve their creator now and for all eternity. That is an incomparable good for those who attain it.

One may still ask why humans do evil; but that question is more properly directed to ourselves than to God. The explanation lies within the human psyche, and not as part of its created nature but as a self-inflicted wound. The question 'why does a man act badly?' is ambiguous. One may mean to ask why some particular individual acted wrongly on some occasion, and then look for special motives operating at that time. Alternatively the question may ask why human beings tend to act badly. The second question evidently seeks a general answer beyond particular motives, and it is likely to look for this in common if not universal features of human beings as such. It was in response to this question that Greek and Roman philosophers began to develop accounts of a tendency in the human soul to pull away from the true and the good and to head towards the deceptive and the vicious. And it is in response to precisely the same question that, beginning with St Paul, Christian thinkers developed the idea of 'original sin'.

Sin is an irreducibly religious concept. There are, of course, non-religious uses of the term, as when a menu announces a 'sinful sundae', or it is said that not to take advantage of an opportunity would be a 'sin'. These, though, are derived meanings indicating indulgent pleasure and culpable omission. Understood in its proper sense, however, sin is a moral evil in its aspect of being an offence against God. It is acting at odds with and in opposition to the divine goodness as expressed in the general creation or in particular commands. Putting it in this abstract way one may be none the wiser as to what kind of action would be sinful. Apart from this problem of *content*, which will be solved by seeing the meaning and value of creation and by discerning any divine laws, there is also a subtler problem of *form*. Evidently, I may disrupt a plan by accident and be quite beyond blame. Or I may act in opposition to a scheme, again not knowing that I am doing so. In this case, however, I may be culpable, perhaps because I ought to have known better, or because I was generally ill-intentioned while not appreciating the particular character of my wrongdoing. In making sense of the idea of sin it is important not to deceive oneself with the comforting but self-serving notion that something could only be sinful if it was done with the explicit intention of giving offence to God.

If the latter were required, then no doubt there would be

few sins to worry about. Yet even the most uncritical apologists for humanity cannot plausibly deny that aggression, avarice, cruelty, lust and culpable stupidity are responsible for injustices and other evils. If we think that those who act in such ways are culpable, then religiously-speaking that will be enough to identify these as sins. Christians who do not like to hear this said often quote scripture as saying that we should not judge lest we ourselves be judged (Matthew 7:1), but that injunction was aimed at the tendency to direct criticism against others and not against ourselves, and was also given as a reminder that some aspects of human motivation may be known only to God. Traditional moral theologians wisely distinguish between *objective* sinfulness and *subjective* culpability – the latter referring to the heart that is seen only by God. In recognising this aspect they do not, however, shy away from identifying objectively sinful kinds of action. Nor should we, in our proper efforts to avoid presuming the depth of someone's moral guilt, avoid judging the wrongness of what is done. Loving the sinner as one created by God, in whom grace can yet operate, it is still possible to judge and to hate the sin: indeed it is a duty to do so.

By any sensible estimate, human sin is pervasive: abuse, deceit, degradation, exploitation, infidelity, murder, mutilation are easily identified both in the past and here and now. Some of these are attributable to special features of their perpetrators, to particular depths of vice or general personal corruption. Others seem due to structural tendencies in the human psyche. There are also recurrent trends towards charity, decency and self-sacrifice; but the general moral situation seems to be one in which things are more liable to go wrong than they are to go right. This contrast between person-specific and general-human inclinations is what is meant by the distinction between 'personal' and 'inherited' (or 'original') sin. The latter term relates, of course, to the Genesis story of the fall of Adam and Eve. However little might be made of this as historical narrative it has a compelling religious logic. If there is a good and all-capable God then his creation could only be inherently good. So if we find structural defects, such as general human sin appears to be, then this cannot be attributed to creation as such but must somehow be posterior and extrinsic to it. Since sin is voluntary it cannot be thought to arise from natural processes alone, as might the competition among animals for food and habitation. Rather, it must represent a decision to act in a way which, however agents may describe it to themselves, is objectively wrong.

Once this course has been taken, more and more wrongdoing is liable to ensue as injustices give rise to resentment, retaliation and yet further wrongs, until humankind is *de facto* corrupted, and collectively so mired in sin that each new generation inherits this condition by something analogous to a Lamarckian inheritance of acquired characteristics. Such is at least part of an understanding of original sin. St Augustine remarks that the two principal effects of this self-inflicted wound on the human race are the disturbance of the passions and the darkening of the intellect. It is hard not to believe in the first, whatever one may take its causes to be; and an implication of the second is that we may never adequately understand the condition that produced it. In other words, the best explanation of our failure to comprehend the deepest source of human evil may be that very source: *sin blinds us to itself*. In creating free agents, God created the possibility, but not the necessity, of their voluntarily acting badly and thereby of corrupting themselves and their descendants. But grace can help us identify that wound, mitigate its effects, and ultimately be restored to a state of prelapsarian goodness. The theology of grace has been the subject of much scholarly study, but it is most memorably captured in the words of John Newton's famous hymn:

> T'was grace that taught my heart to fear,
>   and grace my fears relieved,
> How precious did that grace appear,
>   the hour I first believed.
> Through many dangers, toils and snares,
>   I have already come,
> T'is grace that brought me safe thus far,
>   and grace will lead me home.

As regards the operations of nature rather than the actions of free agents, the problem of evil requires a different, though connected, treatment. Here again, I believe, the best account is to be found in the traditions of Eastern and Western Christianity, though again its origins can be traced back to the philosophers of the ancient world and it can also be found in the writings of medieval Islamic and Jewish thinkers.

Earlier I said that evil is real. That is true, but it is necessary to distinguish between the real and the substantial. The hole in my pocket is real, but it is not something additional to the cloth surrounding it. The difference between that hole and an equivalent region of empty space located in mid-air in front of me is that the hole represents an *absence* of something that ought to be present, whereas the empty space is an innocent void. This is one way of introducing the ancient idea that – while not an illusion – evil is not something additional to the things that there are. In the terminology of Augustine and Aquinas, it is a 'privation' or deficiency. At first sight this may seem like a distinction without a difference, but it is both theoretically important and practically useful.

First, it addresses the challenge that if everything that exists is created by God and evils are among the things that exist, then evils are created by God. Some may think this is not a problem, since they believe that the means is justified by the end, and therefore that so long as the good that results from the manufacture of evil ultimately outweighs it, God is justified in creating it. This, however, is doubly unsatisfactory. First, most religious perspectives have been insistent that one may not intend evil. St Paul famously wrote that it would be a scandal if Christians did what their opponents charged them with, namely 'doing evil that good may come of it' (Romans, 3:8). If this is prohibited of lowly creatures then how infinitely more scandalous would it be to think that God himself should cause suffering for the sake of some benefit? Second, it diminishes God's power to suppose that the only way in which he could bring about some good is by doing something bad. In our case that limitation is evident, but we are not omniscient and omnipotent and so we sometimes find ourselves with no route to the good save by way of the bad. Morally we should resist that temptation, but if we fail we should not console ourselves with the fantasy that 'even God' faces such unhappy choices. God is by definition *almighty*; nothing impedes his will and nothing can tempt him to act badly. To suppose otherwise is a kind of idolatry: thinking of God as a character more at home in a science-fiction extravaganza than as the transcendent focus of religious aspiration.

Second, the idea that natural evil (and moral evil, too) is a lack of what should be present is diagnostically insightful. Using it we can understand the world better, and more effectively direct our own efforts to improve it. Aquinas observes that the generation of one thing is the perishing of another. He means that, in any change, the coming to be of one thing or feature is *ipso facto* the ceasing to be of a previously existing one. If in an effort to improve the illumination of a room I paint the grey walls white, then the coming to be of whiteness is at the expense of the existence of greyness. If a large fish eats a small fish then the latter's loss is the former's gain; and the matter that constituted the sardine, say, now goes to constitute the mackerel. As cells mutate and a cancer develops, one kind of tissue grows at the expense of another. In each case we can say that what from the point of view of the previously existing thing 'ought to be' is now lacking; but that from the point of view of what replaces it there is evident gain.

So put, this may suggest that there can be no absolute evil, or evil *per se*, for every kind of loss is matched by an acquisition. That is not right, however, for consistent with the gain/loss equation is a different calculation implicit in at least some of the examples given, namely that of what ought to be more generally. In my painting of the room grey lost out to white, but we can ask whether that was the right outcome. Let us assume that it was, then no badness was involved, since what, objectively speaking, ought to be (the white) is, and what is not (the grey) ought not to be. In fact, had the grey persisted, *that* would have been a privation of what was needed. In the case of the cancer, the regular tissue's loss was the tumour's gain, but here we want to say that this is bad because it induces all sorts of privations in the body, leading, perhaps, to the ultimate privation: that of life itself. In the case of the fish, we might judge that one state of affairs is better than another if we had some hierarchy of fishy-being that showed mackerel to be existentially superior to sardines. If we have no hierarchy, we can at least say that the loss of life of one fish is not without compensation: being is undiminished, it is only relocated.

What this suggests is that where we are apt to see loss and to speak of evil we should look to discern what else may have come into being and then judge whether all things considered that may not be for the better, if not for the best. Often the answer should be that the gain was of a lesser sort. The thriving virus accompanying the death of the child is not a transaction to which we should be indifferent; nor that of the tumour at the expense of the brain. On the contrary, we should seek to intervene. Few would disagree, but I doubt that so many would embrace the philosophical implication of these judgments: either our favouring of one thing over another is unprincipled partisanship, or else it really is the case that some things are better than others. I hesitated to make a judgment about the greater being of mackerel in comparison to sardines; but I have no hesitation in judging between the flourishing of a virus and of a human being. This verdict squares better with some religious views than with others. In particular the Judaeo-Christian tradition does not hesitate to rank creation and to place mankind high in the order of beings. Men really are better than beetles, and whatever may be God's fondness for the latter it does not amount to placing them higher in creation. An implication of taking this ranking seriously is that one should not be unwilling to see some things perish for the sake of others. Blindness is not a thing in and of itself, but is a lack of sight arising from other absences, themselves explicable in terms of other presences. The eye surgeon interferes with those other presences, such as opaque or inert tissue, in an effort to promote sight; and so, in general, he should.

Why creation should feature such privations is in some

respects a mystery, not least because we are unable to see the depth and breadth of the goodness realised by creation (as well as the extent of evil itself). We can at least see, however, that privations are not directly attributable to creation, for they are not among the things that exist, but instead follow in consequence from them. This excuses God from the immediate charge of having *created* evil, but it does not acquit him from the complaint of foreseeably allowing it to arise and even to flourish. To block this challenge the theist may respond with two points. First, by repeating the lesson of the earlier discussion of gain and loss, namely that the generation of goods is necessarily at the cost of what they replace. In short, any dynamic material creation must involve perishing as well as coming to be. Second, by noting that the atheist has to show that the evils consequent on the existence of substantial being outweigh its goodness. It is hard to see how in principle that could be demonstrated. In fact the consensus of human judgment on the matter favours the verdict that, overall, things are for the good. There are, though, avowed dissenters from this view, whose position is evidently tragic: for, taking the presumed surfeit of evil to show that there is no God, they cannot then pray that the misery will be brought to an end.

Such comfort as these reflections may provide is more likely to appeal to the intellect than to the heart and soul. It is appropriate to end, therefore, by forging a link between this response to the problem of natural evil and the earlier discussion of the challenge of moral evil. The latter led to the introduction of the idea of grace as a divine gift bestowed upon fallen mankind. Grace is no less important in coping with natural evil, for several reasons. First, pain, suffering and adversity often worsen us not just physically but spiritually, making us resentful and embittered and thereby apt to be sinful; hence, we need grace to save us from that corruption. Second, however, suffering can also be an occasion of profound spiritual growth, transforming our evaluations and leading us to see what really matters. Grace can assist and perfect that movement towards wisdom. Third, it has often been observed that the deepest kind of privation that can overtake the lives of humans is not physical but moral and spiritual. Socrates observed that it was better to suffer evil than to inflict it. In a more evidently religious key, Christ taught that the worst that can befall a man is the loss of his soul. Here philosophy and religion converge in the recognition that the deepest problem of evil is the *moral* one. But whereas philosophy can only recognise the fact, religion has an efficacious answer to it in the form of grace. To put this another way, and somewhat paradoxically, while the atheist can either deny the existence of evil or merely record the fact of it, only the theist can provide an explanation and an answer to it. The problem of evil is not the undoing of all religion. Rather, some (but not all) religions offer a solution to the problem of evil: namely, that only grace has brought us safe thus far, and only grace can lead us home.

4

Religion and the Meaning of History

> We can no longer have recourse to the grand narratives
> – we can resort neither to the dialectic of spirit, nor
> even to the emancipation of humanity.
> Jean-François Lyotard

Moral good and evil come in different forms: personal, social, institutional, cultural, political and religious. In trying to understand evil I have suggested that besides looking to particular circumstances and motivations one also needs to acknowledge the general human liability to go morally wrong. In line with the further claim that while evil is certainly real it consists in deficiencies or privations, we should be able to understand both particular and general moral wrongs as involving the absence of what reason, emotion and volition should have established or preserved. Abuse or unfaithfulness in personal relationships involve defects of character on the part of the wrongdoer and inflict (de)privations on the injured party. Institutional injustice involves a want in the allocation of goods due to some, and thus represents a failure of reason and an imposition of loss. The cultural corruption marked by the spread of pornography and the rise of trash TV involves a systematic failure of good judgment and a loss of the sense of social responsibility on the part of media owners, producers, distributors, participants and consumers, with consequent further damage to the fabric of human sentiments: where there should be sensitivity, delicacy and discernment there is coarseness and distraction.

In moving from individual to social evils our vision of the impediments to human flourishing is broadened; but there is a further dimension to be taken account of, the appreciation of which promises to enrich our comprehension of the human condition and the contribution of religious ideas to that understanding. This is the dimension of *history*, understood not just as a sequence of events but as a possibly meaningful narrative: an account not just of what has happened but an interpretative explanation of why things have gone as they have and how they should go in the future (the 'should' here being both predictive and normative). We have already touched on this: first in chapter 2 when discussing the issue of 'presentism', and again in the previous chapter when considering the idea of 'original sin' as some kind of inheritance of acquired moral characteristics. There is more to be said, however, about understanding human existence in its historical dimension than merely observing this trans-generational defect. For one thing, the larger story should have something to say about the good side of things. For another, it may also identify events and trends that have special meaning, which is not the same as assuming that historical development is a sequence of eras, let alone assuming that the present is especially significant.

In the sentence that heads this chapter, Lyotard insists, like other postmodernists, that we should abandon meta-narratives, overarching accounts of events that subsume other more local narratives such as periodic or political histories. In particular, we are to reject the belief that there is anything to be said that might constitute the 'human story'. By contrast, I side with the modernists and the pre-modernists who, in different ways, see deep significance in the broad sweep of history, as well as in the recurrent longings in generations of individuals. That said, I certainly agree with postmodernists when they observe the confusing diversity of interests, cultural forms and lifestyles that characterise economically and technologically advanced societies, but I see this within a larger picture which gives it a meaning that the postmodernists cannot see, and which, given their theoretical commitments, they could not acknowledge even if it seemed apparent to them. Given that postmodernity is a relatively recent condition, it remains to be determined whether human beings can thrive without an ennobling conception of their own nature and destiny. I doubt that they can, though here I am more concerned to identify and defend such a conception than to predict the consequences of living without it or any other meta-narrative.

As we shall see, however, these two issues cannot be wholly separated, for it is characteristic of religious meta-narratives that they imply that failing to observe them is likely to bring us to disaster.

On the morning of 11 September, I walked from Arlington, a Virginia suburb of Washington, DC, across the Key Bridge over the Potomac river and up the hill to Georgetown University where I had recently taken up a visiting professorship. With summer yielding to autumn, the sticky Washington heat had given way to radiant warmth and clear blue skies. From the bridge one can see the Gothic towers of the University on the hill, and in the distance glimpses of some of the symbols of America's affluence and power: the Washington Monument, the Kennedy Center and the Pentagon. I reached my office, and within minutes learned of the first terrorist attack on the World Trade Center. Events moved quickly: news spread of the Pentagon attack and it was reported that another plane was on its way to strike at the White House. The air was cleared of commercial craft and a fighter roared across the sky. Georgetown closed and hundreds of University and Government workers began the walk back across the Potomac – this time seeing smoke billowing up from the Pentagon and spreading to mist across the Virginia sky. A new phase of American history had begun.

The quickest route from the University to the Key Bridge is down a steep and narrow set of steps whose image is well known thanks to the 1973 film *The*

Exorcist, in which they claim the deaths of two characters. Much has been written in analysis of the film and of William Blatty's novel on which it was based. In one obvious respect they concern demonic possession, in another they represent the continuation of a cosmic war between good and evil begun with Lucifer's fall and brought to Earth with the corruption of man. It is a common part of this latter meta-narrative that men and women are used by the force of evil to subvert the sense of their own human nature and value. At one point in Blatty's novel (but not in the de-theologised film), the two Jesuit exorcists, Fathers Merrin and Karras, are in conversation about Regan, the helpless 12-year-old possessed by demons. Karras, the younger priest whose own faith has been waning, asks the older one: 'Why this girl? It makes no sense!' Father Merrin responds: 'I think the point is to make us despair – to see ourselves as animal and ugly; to reject the possibility that God could love us'.

The question of whom God loves (and of whether some are beyond such love) was raised implicitly by both attackers and victims on 11 September. The Key Bridge is named for Francis Scott Key, author of 'The Star-Spangled Banner', the US national anthem. Key's poem was written on 14 September 1814 to celebrate the defence of Baltimore against the British after their burning of Washington. Two centuries later, following only the second foreign attack on DC, those hurrying onto the Bridge from the Georgetown side passed a small garden with a plaque bearing part of Key's verse. Some may even have paused to read it: 'Then conquer we must, when our cause it is just/And this be our motto: "In God is our Trust!"' In the following days the anthem was sung with ever greater feeling, and the stars and stripes were everywhere to be seen, often accompanied by the slogan, 'God Bless America.' Though sometimes voiced in humble and even fearful petition, this seemed more to be a reminder of a long established association between God and the United States. Key's poem displays that same combination of patriotism and belief in God's favour and protection (this is the whole of the last stanza):

> Oh, thus be it ever when free men shall stand
> Between their loved homes and war's desolation;
> Blest with victory and peace, may the Heaven-rescued
> land
> Praise the Power that has made and preserved us a
> nation!
> Then conquer we must, when our cause it is just
> And this be our motto: 'In God is our trust!'
> And the star-spangled banner in triumph shall wave
> O'er the land of the free and the home of the brave!

It is part of this self-conception that America sees its destiny in quasi-Biblical terms: as a fruitful land given to a godly people and to their descendants in return for their fidelity, rather as God covenanted with Abra(ha)m: 'I will keep my promise to you and to your descendants in future generations. I will be your God and the God of your descendants. I will give to you and to your descendants this land' (Genesis 17:7). Besides shock and rage, many Americans registered incomprehension of the possibility that others might regard them as an ungodly or un-virtuous people. In a rare exception to the general presumption of blamelessness, the Christian evangelist Pat Robertson incurred the wrath of critics by suggesting that perhaps American sinfulness had led God to lower his protective arm from around the nation. Within a day or so, however, he felt compelled to apologise. But given a Biblical mentality his was an intelligible response, for the analogy with the chosen people of scripture, the Israelites, would lead to the thought that when death is visited upon the nation it is because of its infidelity and sinfulness. Certainly that is a central theme of Jewish sacred history; and Robertson and the like-minded may have been thinking of the penalties of disobedience listed in Deuteronomy 28: 'If you do evil and reject the Lord he will bring on you disaster … and will give your enemies victory over you.'

Though they certainly never shared the view of America as a people in covenant with God, the attackers of 11 September and their leadership used scriptural language to denounce the United States as the 'Great Satan' and to justify violence against it. In this they followed the example of the late Ayatollah ('Sign of God') Ruhollah Khomeini. Watching the Twin Towers burn and then crash down, the symbolism seemed inescapable, and it is hard not to imagine how it was interpreted among some religiously inspired groups. Here I am not thinking of the magazine article purporting to show the sneering face of Satan in the black clouds billowing from the Twin Towers, but of a more ancient literary source. It is customary for 'peoples of the book' to identify Babylon as a place of human vanity and ungodliness. In Genesis 11, we read this:

> [T]he people of the whole world had only one language and used the same words … and they came to a plain in Babylonia and settled there. They said to one another … let us build a city with a tower that reaches to the sky, so that we can make a name for ourselves … Then the Lord came down to see the city and the tower which they had built and he said: 'These are all one people and they speak one language; this is just the beginning of what they are going to do. Soon they will be able to do anything they want!' … So the Lord scattered them over the Earth.

One of the principal targets of Arab critics of the United States, more damnable for many than its support of Israel, is what is seen as America's cultural and economic imperium, lately veiled under the guise of 'globalisation'. This is objected to by Islamists and secularists alike, but while the complaint certainly has a political aspect, it also has a deep religious foundation in Islam's understanding of history and of its place in the world. It is important to appreciate the latter points or else one will be led to suppose that Arab-Islamic anti-

Americanism is just a desert-heated version of the resentment of American cultural expansion felt by some in Eastern and Western Europe, India, South East Asia and South America. Increasingly it seems that the people of the world have one (main) language, American English; and that across the globe cities are being built with towers reaching to the sky in emulation of Lower Manhattan. Unlike minarets erected to broadcast the Muslim call to prayer, which are thus a visual symbol of Islamic worship, as in the Christian world is the church spire, these new towers do not point to Heaven but betoken the pursuit of earthly values which they also celebrate. To that extent they risk being idols.

Famously, Muslims share with Jews an abhorrence of that particular offence to God. Moses warns the people: 'Obey his command not to make yourselves any kind of idol, because the Lord your God is like a flaming fire; he tolerates no rivals' (Deuteronomy 4:23). Not only is America the model for others, it is often the major investor: putting money, products and personnel into developing regions, again and again making a name for itself and in the process encouraging others to do likewise. The words 'this is just the beginning of what they are going to do. Soon they will be able to do anything they want' could be those of an editorial in a nationalist or other newsletter bemoaning the spread of the American imperium. To people familiar with scriptural styles of heavenly disapprobation and taken with their own prophetic mission, God's judgment on Babylon may

seem to add a further charge to the accumulated griev-
ances of America's Islamist critics.

Before 11 September, Osama bin Laden, the spiritual
leader of al-Qaida, was quoted as having said: 'The
serpent is America, and we have to stop them. We have to
cut off the head of the snake. We cannot let the American
army into our area.' Here he is referring principally to
Saudi Arabia, the country of his birth and, more importantly, the Muslim Holy Land of Mecca and Medina.
America's military presence there during the Gulf War
was doubly offensive to bin Laden, for beyond the fact
that the prophet said that no non-Muslims should tread
holy soil, America used the Holy Land to launch its attack
upon Iraq, a part of the world associated with Islam's
greatest cultural achievements, particularly in Baghdad.
In a video released to the media after the New York and
Washington attacks, bin Laden spoke as follows:

> Our Islamic nation has been tasting the same [horror]
> for more than 80 years: humiliation and disgrace, its
> sons killed and their blood spilled, its sanctities dese-
> crated ... [Now] God has blessed a group of vanguard
> Muslims, the leading edge of Islam, to destroy America
> ... when the sword fell upon America after 80 years,
> hypocrisy raised its head up high, bemoaning the killers
> who played with the blood, honour and sanctities of
> Muslims ... I tell the [apostates] these events have
> divided the world into two camps: the faithful and the
> infidels. Now every Muslim must rise to defend his reli-
> gion. The winds of faith and of change are blowing to
> remove evil from the land of Mohammed, peace be

upon him. As for America … it will not live in peace before peace reigns in Palestine, and before all the army of the infidels depart the land of Mohammed, peace be upon him.

These words are evidently intended to be heard as right-eous and prophetic. For the occasion of delivering them, bin Laden dressed himself as a *majhoud*, a holy warrior, donning a combat jacket over customary Afghan reli-gious garb. Speaking a high form of Arabic laced with Qur'anic and other Islamic references, he aims to recall the Bedouin tribes who are reputed to have spread Islam throughout and beyond Arabia in the century following Mohammed's death in 632. The repeated mention of 80 years is a reference back to the defeat of the Ottoman Empire at the hands of the French and the British in 1918. Besides occupying the ancient imperial capital of Constantinople and partitioning the lands, the Western imperialists held captive the Ottoman Sultan, who as well as being a political leader was regarded as the Caliph or universal head of Sunni Islam (about 90 per cent of the world's Muslims). Although the Turks subsequently liberated the country, the movement that achieved this was a secular one and it abolished the Sultanate in 1922, ending the Caliphate two years later. In effect, then, 1918 brought to an end 1300 years of an Islamic political-religious identity under the governance of a series of Caliphs descending from the period of the prophet himself.

Few Muslims seriously aspire to see the restoration of

the Caliphate, but that does not mean that its destruction is viewed with indifference, or that the circumstances of its ending are not recalled with resentment. Bin Laden's ire against the 'hypocrites' and 'apostates' is likewise calculated to resonate with Arab Muslims. Those accused are Arab states viewed as the West's allies (Egypt, Jordan, Saudi Arabia), with the charge of apostasy adding a special threat, since in Islamic law apostates must be killed. The reference to the division of the world into the 'camps of the faithful' and of 'the infidels' again refers back to an historic Muslim idea and offers the prospect of large and more widespread conflict. The distinction adverted to is that between *Dar al-Islam* (the camp, or sphere, of Islam) and *Dar al-Harb* (the camp, or sphere, of war). Like the image of the *majhoud*, these derive from the period of original Muslim expansion in the seventh and eighth centuries. Being the universal truth for mankind, Islam seeks converts. Indeed, the prophet laid upon his followers the duty of *jihad* (struggling in and on behalf of the path of God). Consequently the distinction between that part of the world in which Muslim governance and law prevail and that part in which they do not is as much a theological as a socio-geographical one. Certainly it has clear implications for action: just as in the original Islamic expansion, true Muslims must promote the faith in those parts that are not as yet within the camp of Islam. Being the place of striving, this other world of infidels is also the place of *jihad*, the sphere of war.

Understandably, President Bush and Prime Minister

Blair have repeated and emphasised the claim that the war against terrorism launched in response to 11 September is not a campaign directed against Arabs or Muslims more generally and that it has no cultural or ideological dimension. They see it instead as an intense though narrowly focused response to a small number of shallowly rooted terrorists; cowardly fanatics whose message has nothing to do with the true spirit of Islam. So put, things look fairly simple and one dimensional. A bunch of fanatics flew planes into buildings in New York and Washington because of their resentment of America's economic power and influence, and its support of Israel. The only values in conflict are those of security, liberty and toleration, as against violence, tyranny and coercion.

It is significant that this political account makes no reference to history or religion. No doubt that is partly deliberate, since these are recognised to be powerful motives and the US/British effort must be to contain the conflict, not extend it. So far as our understanding of the events is concerned, however, it is essential to consider the various narratives that give them meaning for both perpetrators and victims. Placing them in such contexts is also relevant to the evaluation of what kind of evil they represent. In the most ordinary secular narrative a group of extremists struck a devastating blow against the world's superpower and occasioned a new wave of American political and military activity. In a more abstract account it might be said that this was a major event in a developing conflict between open, liberal democracy, and representatives of essentially pre-modern, illiberal regimes that are contemptuous of human rights. Whether put in these terms or in others more favourable to al-Qaida's view, the clash is between political ideologies about which one cannot be neutral, hence the challenge heard on both sides: 'either you are with us or you are against us – there is no middle ground.'

Moving into a religious key the question raised by Pat Robertson's response now becomes unavoidable: is it the case that America has stood in some quasi-covenantal relationship with the deity, in which he has protected and blessed it for so long as the nation was godly and goodly? If so, what does 11 September say about the state of that covenant: is it still preserved or has it been irre-vocably breached? In either case, what was America's sinfulness, and how can the nation hope to be absolved from this? Switching now to Osama bin Laden's perspec-tive, the attacks are one day's raids in a holy war. That war is hallowed, having been launched by Mohammed and his followers when they set out from Madinat an-Nabi (Medina), the 'City of the Prophet', first capturing Mecca, then advancing through and beyond Arabia. *Jihad* is divinely sanctioned, and the striving cannot end until the world of Islam is co-extensive with the world itself. While the Jewish state of Israel, and the American pres-ence in the Middle East are both to be eliminated, that is not an end in itself but an important part of the restoration of Islamic rule in the Holy Lands of Arabia and Palestine, preparatory to consecrating the whole Earth through its conversion to Islam. In this respect bin Laden's prayerful hope is parallel to that of traditional Christians. A significant difference, however, is that whatever the actual behaviour of Christians, their bloody warfare has no support in Christian scripture.

The ultimate story in this series of narratives is that explored by Blatty in *The Exorcist*: not the particularities of demonic possession, but the larger cosmic battle between supernatural good and evil. Notwithstanding the idiocy of the tabloid cover showing the sneering face of Satan in the Twin Tower inferno, it ill behoves either Christians or Muslims, committed as they are to the reality of the spiritual, to reject the possibility that human events are caught up in a supernatural opposition. Both traditions offer mythic accounts of the banishment of a former angel: in Christianity *Lucifer* is expelled from Heaven, in Islam *Iblis* is exiled from *janna*, 'the Garden'. In each case the evil one embarks on a campaign of opposition to the divine plan and ends up being named as Satan (*Shaytaan*), the 'adversary' of God and man.

Here it is important to bear in mind two points. First, the philosophical account of evil as privation or defect in no way diminishes its reality or force. Unwarranted discontent, jealous hatred, and unjustified resentment are powerful motives, and when conjoined with the knowledge that efforts to gratify them face inevitable frustration, the evil is deepened. Second, the metaphysical question of whether there is in fact a conflict within creation, involving one or more spiritual beings made evil by its free choices, needs to be distinguished from the matter of whether the various mythic representations are true, or were ever intended to be understood literally. Satan is not identified explicitly in the Hebrew Bible until First Chronicles, where he is introduced as 'wanting to bring trouble on the people of Israel', and the familiar mythic devilish features such as are depicted in the magazine image have no Biblical source. Nonetheless, it is a central element of these faiths that evil is a reality. Accepting this, and the existence of the spiritual realm, there is no evident absurdity in the idea that there are immaterial beings acting in opposition to God, inflicting privations on humankind, in part by corrupting them, just as some humans corrupt others both directly, through personal influence, and indirectly, through social, institutional, cultural, political and religious structures.

The publication of Blatty's novel in 1971 and the release of the film in 1973 came in a period in which China was undergoing the Cultural Revolution with enormous costs to Buddhism and Christianity; in the Holy Land Jews and Muslims were at war; Hindus and Muslims were in conflict over Bangladesh; in Ulster Catholics and Protestants were killing one another in increasing terror; America was counting the human and moral cost of the Vietnam War, and suffering the shock of the Arab oil embargo, and in Washington itself lawful governance was shown to have been corrupted in the Watergate affair. Against this background the idea that forces of evil, additional to individual human malefactors, are at work in the world particularly disrupting and perverting the religious quest, has a certain intelligibility. Certainly Blatty meant his readers to reflect on this possibility. If such an account can identify a supernatural dimension in the events of its time, then a similar story might be told about the events of 11 September. Also, it is not one that is available only to Christians, for anyone who believes in the possibility of supernatural evil might well think that the events of that date are of a diabolical sort. Here one might echo and add to the words of Merrin the exorcist: the point may be to make us despair – to see human beings as animal and ugly; to reject the possibility that God could love them and to reject even the possibility that there is a caring God.

The last narrative I have sketched is about as 'meta' as things can get. Whether it strikes readers as being plausible is of less concern than that the idea, range and power of meta-narratives in general should have been communicated. After all, even if such accounts of supernatural conflict, or of Islam's historic mission, or of America's divine protection, or, for that matter, of ideological conflict between post-enlightenment liberal democracy, and dark, pre-modern illiberality, is false, there are many who believe and are animated by them. Merely to observe this, however, fails to engage the challenge that no one *should* believe meta-narratives of any kind, since they are part of a discredited past which we have many good reasons to leave behind us. As the postmodernist opponent of edifying or terrifying tales may note with self-irony, this at least is an aspect of human thought in which we can discern some historical progress.

There are two kinds of opposition to viewing the lives of society and of human beings in general, in terms of historical and ideological grand narratives. First, there is the objection of the pragmatists. Like Blair, Bush and other 21st-century leaders, they emphasise the idea that politics should be about making people's lives better in ways that are uncontroversial, through improving accountability, oversight, efficiency and standards of service in the public sector, and by promoting comparable virtues in the private sector. This approach tends to conflate the identities and roles of citizens and consumers. Whatever personal attachments and convictions participants may have are recognised to be important in motivating them, but are not taken as defining parts of the common moral, religious or ideological project of society – for there is none. Though it may be true that individuals and groups share common interests, and even that everyone wants 'the same thing', these interests have no deep philosophical significance, and the universal goal is only the formal one that 'things go well'. From this point of view, the idea of ideologically-motivated policy-making, and, *a fortiori*, of policies which seek to implement some general philosophical view, are both irrelevant to the new politics, and are the obvious curse of the old. The collapse of Communism, and the move to the political centre, both mark the failure of ideology and the success of 'realism'.

As I have described it, this view of progress is non-theoretical, or only minimally theoretical. It is meant to correspond to what anyone with even the most modest knowledge of 20th-century history, and a modicum of common sense, should accept. Sometimes it adds a few rhetorical flourishes, appealing to the advance of technology and the 'challenges and opportunities' presented by the new information systems; but in essence it is wary of casting its message in the language of historical narratives. The fact that to do the latter would involve a kind of contradiction – saying in effect that 'the big story is that there are no big stories' – encourages the more self-reflective not to speak in these terms, and just to say that we are no longer ideological. This escapes paradox, but makes it hard to see why the current situation should count as progress. To put it another way, since it is clearly being assumed that all this does indeed represent progress, the question arises of what conception of human life, value and meaning lies behind the judgment that things are getting better.

While it is open to the pragmatist to eschew any philosophy of history, to the extent that he refuses it, his account of the good of present day social existence must seem shallow. By contrast, the view of avowed ideological progressives seems more coherent, for they locate their analysis of the present within a larger account of the significance of history. Famously this was the mode of Marx who wrote of 'all history [being] the history of class struggle' and saw the movement of historical forces as leading to perfect justice as social arrangements attained to a proper harmony of purpose, activity and fulfilment. This image was part of a synoptic vision of history as a whole, a general style of thinking that Marx derived from Hegel, who termed it 'world history'. But while Hegel was content to understand the dialectic of history, and to observe with satisfaction the ascent of 'Spirit' or 'Reason' within it, Marx was increasingly concerned to accelerate a process of political revolution and sought to use philosophy as a means of advancing this. Thus his move from a speculative or 'scientific' idea of philosophy to a practical or 'political' one, well-captured in his much-quoted claim that while 'philosophers have only interpreted the world in various ways, the point is to change it'.

Philosophical history sees the task of the theorist as being to make sense of the past by discerning significant patterns within it. Since it will be a mark of a theoretician's greatness that he sees patterns not hitherto observed, or if observed not yet adequately understood, it is likely that he will also be conceptually creative in coming up with new styles of description and explanation. One such notion is the broad Hegelian concept of the 'dialectic of history', in which lived ideas are seen to have come into contradiction and then to have been abandoned by being transformed through synthesis. Others are the Marxist concepts of 'class struggle' and 'the alienation of labour from the process of production'. As these last examples remind us, the major legacy of Hegelian world history is socialist political analysis. But this is not the only, or most recent influential expression of the idea that history is leading somewhere and that the principal manifestation of this movement is political.

The fact that Francis Fukuyama's book *The End of History and the Last Man* (1992) occasioned so much interest is evidence, I believe, of the perennial power of historical meta-narratives. The point of the title, as of that of the essay from which it derived, 'The End of History?' (1989), was not to suggest that no further large or important events were going to happen. Hence Fukuyama is not refuted by the catalogue of dramatic world events that have occurred in the last decade. Rather, his thesis was that whatever occurred would do so within a context that constituted the completion of an extended historical movement. He was, as he said, 'raising once again the question of whether there is such a thing as a Universal History of mankind', and then not only answering affirmatively, but saying what the end point of that directional history consists in. In one respect Fukuyama's answer was, like Marx's, economic; but in another it was also, like Hegel's, moral. The end of history, in Fukuyama's account, consists in the achievement of liberal democracy converged on by interconnected movements. These movements are in part the result of ideological evolution and in part of scientific innovation and advance. The application of modern natural science has affected societies by presenting the possibilities of advanced military capacity and enhanced economic production. While all can benefit from these, there is a comparative advantage to capitalist economies in which movements of investment and labour are relatively unencumbered. Wishing to improve and protect these resources and the fruits of their deployment, capitalist societies also have a special interest in developing military and other technologies. Thus the dynamic of scientific/technological movement is inherently progressive.

This of itself, however, is insufficient to produce political liberty, and so an additional historical explanation is needed to account for the widespread aspiration to liberal democracy. Here Fukuyama achieves both a further distancing from Marx and a closer approximation to Hegel. Not only does he see the economic motor of historical change leading to capitalism rather than to socialism, but he sees the economic account as necessarily incomplete in view of the moral dimension of human nature. Following Hegel, he holds that as well as having material needs, men have a profound desire to be acknowledged as beings of value and dignity, and beyond that to have the same recognition accorded to the people and things which they most deeply value. In connection with these desires we are subject to a range of powerful emotions: *anger* at being disrespected, *shame* at failure to live up to our own worth, and *pride* at being judged according to it. Again Fukuyama follows Hegel by seeing the desire for recognition as explaining the direction of political history – a history brought to completion by the establishment (at least in theory) of a system of universal and reciprocal recognition. As Fukuyama puts it, 'Liberal democracy replaces the irrational desire to be recognised as greater than others with a rational desire to be recognised as equal'. What is true of individuals is true of societies as a whole. And seeing the advantages of liberty, security and wealth, others in the world aspire to this condition also. The end point of ideological evolution has been identified; liberal democracy obtains in an increasing number of economically forward-moving societies; and this political and economic combination is aspired to by those in other parts: we can say that this is where history was trying to get to, and that it has arrived there.

Unsurprisingly, Fukuyama has been criticised by opponents of capitalism and by critics of the values of liberal democracy. Environmentalists, pacifists, anti-globalists, communitarians, socialists and traditional conservatives can all find reason to take issue with both the details and the spirit of his analysis. For the reasons given above, pragmatists are not quite sure what attitude to take. On the one hand, they like the vindication of the status quo; on the other, they are troubled by the form of the vindication being itself theoretical and ideological. My interest, however, is in two other responses: that of the postmodernist and that of the traditional theist. Since it may readily be assumed that one point that the former may take issue with is the suggestion that the collapse of Communism marks the triumph of liberal capitalism, it is interesting to note that among the first critics of this idea was Pope John Paul II, a figure who is not only far removed from postmodernist thinking, but who is acknowledged to have himself played an important part in the Communist collapse. On this score, therefore, there may be little to divide the postmodernist and the pre-modernist. Where they will part company, however, is over the matter of whether an account such as Fukuyama's or Marx's or Hegel's is at all credible.

There is obviously a structural analogy between the following claims:

(1) that the direction of history is towards the realisation of free-market, liberal democracy

(2) that the direction of history is towards the realisation of perfect justice through the intermediary of a communist state

(3) that the direction of history is towards the realisation of the total victory of the camp of faithful Islam over the camp of the infidels

(4) that the direction of history is towards the realisation of the kingdom of God in its entirety both on Earth and in Heaven

(5) that the direction of history is towards the full and permanent realisation of the Abrahamic covenant and the completion of God's will for his people.

In each case history is viewed 'teleogically', as oriented and moving towards a certain goal. In the case of claims (3), (4) and (5), it is assumed that this movement is divinely ordained: God is an agent in history moving it is a certain direction. Bearing in mind what was said about evil, this claim will have to be understood in the terms previously described. God does not will evil *per se*, but what he does will may give rise to it, and he may sustain the activities of the evil-doer for the sake of the divine plan. This may be troubling to contemplate and even difficult to comprehend, but those are separate matters from the issue at hand – which is that for the Muslim, Christian and Jewish advocates of (3), (4) and (5) respectively, human history is comprehended in the greatest of all meta-narratives: 'sacred history'.

In the poetic myths of Babylon and other early Near-Eastern societies, as in the creation myths of pre-Hindu cultures in Asia, the course of events as they bear upon human interests was often explained in terms of the special roles and dominions of particular deities. Gods and goddesses of life, fertility and death, and of mountains, valleys, rivers, sea and sky are busy or idle, happy or angry, proximate or remote. Depending on the combination of factors, things happen which men and women have reason to be grateful for or devastated by; but none of this amounts to the notion of creation and providence as these feature in developed monotheism. The God of Judaism, the God of Christianity, and the God of Islam is in each case conceived to transcend the category of objects. God is not another person in the universe distinguished by his immateriality and power, but the beginning and end of everything, bringing all beings into existence out of nothing (*ex nihilo*), and capable of annihilating any and every being – not crushing it to dust or burning it to vapour, but making it and everything else cease. Clearly such a God is related to creation in a special and all-encompassing way. Given this metaphysical fact and the content of revelation as recorded in the Hebrew Bible, believers of all three faiths have reason to look to world history with an eye to its meaning and orientation. Indeed, one of the defining features of the manner in which history is recorded in the Hebrew Bible is the ascription of providential significance.

To the postmodernist, this is just to identify a remote source and model of subsequent secular meta-narratives, such as that of the Renaissance humanist for whom all human effort should aspire to the condition of perfect civilization, or of the Enlightenment rationalist for whom the course of culture leads to self-understanding and autonomy, or of Hegel, or of Marx, or of Fukuyama. On this account, while being less fantastic in disavowing supernatural influences and purposes, these later meta-narratives are no less the product of the illusion of historical meaning. Where religious and philosophical thinkers have seemed to see directionality and significance there are only the fabulous tales that men and women tell themselves. Where once these may have originated in fear of natural forces and the hope of allying oneself with them, now they are part of efforts to generate or maintain social forces.

As well as entertaining the completion of history, Fukuyama wrote of a creature who emerges at its end, the 'last man'. This is a type, modelled after one first conceived by Nietzsche, who through the accordance of universal and equal recognition, and the enjoyment of peace and prosperity, loses the desire to establish himself as standing above the equalising norms of liberal democracy. Fukuyama envisages a situation in which, seeing this possibility in prospect, men draw back from the course of history even to the point of reasserting themselves as 'first men' once again battling for power and prestige. Setting aside the question of whether this provides a diagnosis of political and social violence, it may seem as though here, at least, there is a convergence of concepts. For, to the postmodernist, all men are 'first men', and all human life is a continuous struggle for superiority, a struggle often concealed by the rhetoric of progressive narratives.

In darker moments this can seem as though it may be true. In lighter ones, it looks as though the world may be in neo-Hegelian ascent such as Fukuyama supposes. These possibilities stand in apparent opposition but there is a way of reconciling them. If Judaeo-Christian sacred history is correct, then the sort of meta-narrative I outlined earlier may make sense of events as great as the collapse of Soviet Communism and as terrible as the attack of 11 September. Mankind's inherited fallenness leads to a darkening of the intellect and a disturbance of the passions which, particularly when raised to social and cultural levels, make great evils possible. At the same time, however, mankind is not created fallen, but is equipped with reason and will directed towards the true and the good in order that he may a play a role in the divine plan for creation. The opposition of these factors may be expected to show itself in the course of events, and the direction of those events may provide some indication of where, at any given time, we have got to in the task of realising God's plan for mankind.

Unless one embraces the nihilism of the postmodernist, then the idea of meta-narratives remains a possibility. But then one must ask what the condition of its possibility is. As Bernard Williams puts it in his recent book *Truth and Truthfulness* (2002): 'there is a large difficulty in principle, that the stories [advanced by teleological histories] need a mechanism to explain how such a process could be possible.' In order to see 'direction' in history, Marx and Hegel tried to find substitutes for providence. It is doubtful, however, whether anything short of real purposeful agency can provide history with a teleology. If that is right, and if the idea of a meta-narrative has rational appeal, then so should the notion that ultimately the course of human history is a religious one, a movement towards or away from God.

5

Religion, Value and Purpose

Judging whether life is or is not worth living amounts to
answering the fundamental question of philosophy.
Albert Camus

The previous chapter pursued the suggestion that only a
religious way of thinking can provide an overarching
account of the meaning of human history, or make sense
of the idea that history may be understood in terms of its
orientation towards some significant end. More needs to
be said about the nature of this idea in order to connect
with the issues of religion and morality, and the link will
come through the notion of personal or existential
meaning.

First, the idea of an 'end' may be interpreted as
marking a cessation, or as identifying a goal; the two of
which come together in the concept of 'completion'.
There is, therefore, a sense in which the claim that events
are proceeding towards an end may be entirely free of
any metaphysical or religious presuppositions: namely,
when all that is being said is that a process is coming to a
point of *cessation*. The processes at work within the Sun
are such as to lead in due course to the destruction of the

solar system. Assuming that nothing interferes, and that human beings are not already extinct long before then, these processes will bring human history to an end (at least in its earthly phase). But they do not in any way constitute a goal for it; and hence, since that is part of the idea of completion, nor will they *complete* human history. Evidently, it is one thing to conceive of beginnings, transitions and endings in terms of a sequence of events; and quite another to conceive of them in the terms of some purpose-revealing narrative, in which they are shown to have the character of origination, development and denouement, or of departure, journey and destination.

The issue, therefore, is whether any sense can be made of the objective meaning or direction of history without some religious assumptions. As was mentioned, Hegel and Marx sought to provide just this: Marx by reference to the operation of historical laws determining economic events (analogous to laws of nature governing physical events); Hegel in terms of the operation of 'Reason' or 'Spirit'. The latter capitalisation indicates that something transcendent of individual minds is intended; and it is well-known that Hegel generally writes of the animating force of history in terms drawn from religious thought. Sometimes this has the flavour of highly abstract theology, as when, in *The Phenomenology of Spirit* (1806), he writes of 'the Absolute Idea being Spirit coming to know itself as Spirit, and as having life, through History'. At other times it has an evangelical character, as when, in the same work, he encourages steadfastness, saying that 'we must hold to the conviction that it is the nature of Truth to prevail when its time has come; and that it appears only when this time has arrived'. Hegel was fully conscious of the religious associations of this language. Indeed, he saw himself as providing a critical and systematic exposition of central metaphysical truths to which, when they wrote of 'creation' and of 'incarnation', the authors of Hebrew and Christian scripture had previously given metaphorical and symbolic expression.

Some Christian philosophers have taken great exception to this. Søren Kierkegaard (1813-55) saw it as revealing of Hegel's lack of religious spirit and of his missing the point of the Judaeo-Christian narrative, that he presented the metaphysics of World History as if it were a mere philosophical thesis and not a call to commitment, and then thought that Christianity could be understood in the same terms. There is something to this criticism. It should also be said, however, that Kierkegaard's preoccupation with individual inner experience, existential self-questioning, and non-rational leaps of faith, is at variance with conceptions of Christianity as being historically developed, socially embodied, rationally warranted and possessed of legitimate teaching authorities. In this respect, at least, Hegel is closer to the great scholastic thinkers such as Aquinas; and it is no surprise, therefore, that Kierkegaard, sometimes known as 'the melancholy Dane', was also hostile to medieval Catholicism. In *Stages on Life's Way* (1845) he has his pseudonymous author, 'Frater Taciturnus', write of 'the darkness of the Middle Ages, the intolerable Roman yoke, the papal power with its nightmare pressed on consciences'.

My concern, however, is with a different problem faced by Hegel and others who appropriate the structure and language of religious meta-narratives when setting down their own demythologised accounts. In essence it is a simple dilemma: either such accounts are genuinely free of religious assumptions, in which case they can be purged of talk of 'Mind', 'Reason' or 'Spirit', 'animating', 'directing' and even 'entering' human history; or else they rely essentially on these concepts, and therefore must be taken as purporting to describe some religious/metaphysical reality. If the latter, then they are not alternatives to sacred history, but versions of it. If the former, then let us see the unqualifiedly secular versions. Some try to discharge this obligation. I have already mentioned Marx, who succeeded Hegel; but an equally interesting example is Giambattista Vico (1688-1744). Where Marx was to see all history as a conflict between labourers and owners over the means of production, Vico viewed all individual and social histories as corresponding to patterns of rising, growing to maturity, declining and falling. As it happens, Vico was also a Christian, but religious ideas are arguably inessential to his account of historical understanding; certainly this account was adopted by non-believers. In *The New Science* (1725), Vico distinguishes between *the natural order*, which we cannot understand, and *the order of human affairs*, which we can. That difference of intelligibility lies in the fact that whereas nature is independent of us, and opaque to our gaze, human history is a *product* of human interests and motives, and is transparent to studied reflection.

In this respect, then, both Vico and Marx may be said to discharge the obligation to provide a meta-narrative that is not essentially religious, but they do so by saying that, in one way or another, the story is one of our own making. Such meanings, purposes and direction as human history may appear to exhibit, are ones that human beings have put there. This may make for interesting cultural studies, but it no more provides the idea of an unchosen objective goal of human existence than the record of where a traveller *has been* provides an account of what his destination *should be*, or provides grounds for determining whether his journeying so far has had any real point or purpose. Records of human behaviour, even if they show it to correspond to recurrent patterns, are not an account of the meaning and purpose of human existence *per se*. In fairness to Vico, however, he also believed that behind these patterns, as behind the regularities of nature, there stands Divine Reason. But, of course, any reliance on this idea to transform pattern into purpose serves to confirm my suggestion that only a religious way of thinking can yield an account of the meaning of human history, or make sense of the idea that it may be understood as being oriented to some significant end.

In *The Myth of Sisyphus* (1942), Albert Camus (1913-60) claims that 'there is but one truly serious philosophical problem, and that is suicide. Judging whether life is or is not worth living amounts to answering the fundamental question of philosophy.' Later, he added that the challenge is to live 'without the aid of eternal values'. Camus's focus is on the question of whether life has meaning. The problem of suicide arises because of a 'total absence of hope' resulting from the confrontation between the 'human need [for answers] and the unreasonable silence of the world'. No doubt there are those to whom it never occurs to raise existential questions, but it is common among intelligent and reflective people to ask whether, beyond the purposes they choose to pursue day to day, and even year to year, there is any objective meaning or goal of human existence. It is this sort of question that Camus has in mind, and it is the sense that the world provides no answer that troubles him. Sometimes he writes as though the existence of God and a divine plan would provide life with the significance it otherwise lacks. Mostly, however, he embraces his own policy of defiance in the face of the absurdity of finding himself asking questions about meaning in a meaningless world. He even comes to the conclusion that 'life will be lived all the better if it has no meaning.' Certainly suicide would bring an end to the absurd, at least as it arises from the confrontation between one's own questioning consciousness and the silent world. But to choose it is to retreat in defeat. Electing to live neither eliminates nor solves the problem of the absurd, but with conscious defiance comes an intensification of life.

This last aspect is reminiscent of the heightened consciousness associated with the recognition of immediate danger. Indeed, the idea that continuous awareness of absurdity might make life worth living is analogous to the thought that a more or less constant adrenaline rush arising from the recognition of the intrinsic pointlessness of the activities that give rise to it would make those activities worth engaging in. It is hard not to see this as self-deceiving. If life really has no meaning, point or value, then there is no meaning, point or value in the excitement attendant on the recognition or acceptance of this fact. On the other hand, if there is something worthwhile in this intensification of lived experience, then it is false that life has no value. The second option suggests an escape from the paradox, since one may now distinguish between deep meaning and the existential thrill of absurdity and then allow that while the world offers no deep meaning it nevertheless provides for existential thrill. The trouble now, however, is with this idea of the thrill of absurdity. First, it is doubtful that many do, or could be brought to feel it. Hence it is liable to be a rare form of relief. Second, it is a poor substitute for deep meaning, being neither deep nor evidently meaningful. Third, it is not clear that it is any more significant than a chemically induced euphoria. Since one can only enjoy intoxication while alive, the possibility of getting drunk offers the same sort of reason not to commit suicide as does the availability of existential thrill. How much of a reason either provides depends on how much of a relief from existential dread each is felt to offer. These being highly subjective matters I leave it to readers to evaluate them for themselves. I only reiterate the point that the thrill of absurdity, like adrenaline rushes and chemically induced euphoria, cannot give life the objective meaning it is deemed to lack. It is dangerous to suppose otherwise, for when the supposition is seen to be illusory, the resulting despair is likely to be all the more acute.

The myth of Sisyphus was well-chosen to illustrate the human problem and its solution as Camus conceives them, but it also exposes the inadequacy of that and similar responses. In consequence of defying the gods, Sisyphus suffered an eternal punishment: to push a boulder to the top of a hill from which it would then roll down again, this to be repeated *ad infinitum*. Notwithstanding the objective pointlessness of the task, he persists in it defiantly. Sisyphus has no hope, but nor does he despair. He goes on pushing, climbing, and descending; choosing not to be undone by his fate but to make it his life. Given this representation of Sisyphus as a heroic creator of the value of his own existence, it is apt to introduce a figure glimpsed at the end of the previous chapter: one who stands behind Camus; whose philosophy of the human condition informed Camus's own; and whose influence on views about religion, World History, personal meaning and human morality has probably been greater than of any other modern atheist thinker: Friedrich Nietzsche (1844-1900).

It is notoriously difficult to say what exactly Nietzsche really believed. This is due in part to his rhetorical and sometimes aphoristic literary modes, and in part to his habit of distancing himself from earlier expressions of his thought. Even the latter tendency has its complications. It is not that he simply renounced or retracted earlier views, as if judging them to be straightforwardly false; rather he suggested that they represented successive personae, responding in different mythic ways to the same dramatic context. This last element provides the fixed point of Nietzsche's turning world; for he insists throughout that the context of his reflections is that of a world absent of God, purpose, meaning and value.

Nietzsche was the son of a Lutheran pastor and was both familiar with the Bible and well-informed about German Protestant theology. In a comment that may have revealed a conflicted spirit, he described himself as having the blood of theologians in his veins. Early in his university studies (if not before), however, he abandoned Christianity and moved toward atheism. Subsequently, he developed a deep criticism of theistic religion, and wrote scathingly of Christianity. His criticisms, however, were more of what theism represented and of what, in particular, this kind of compassionate religion encouraged, than of Christian theology *per se*. Nietzsche's basic attitude is captured in a typically lyrical passage from the

1882 *The Gay Science* or *Joyful Wisdom* (*Die Fröhliche Wissenschaft*). In a section provocatively headed 'The meaning of our cheerfulness', he writes:

> The greatest recent event – that 'God is dead', that the belief in the Christian God has become unbelievable – is already beginning to cast its first shadows over Europe …
>
> Indeed, we philosophers and 'free spirits' feel, when we hear the news that the 'old god is dead', as if a new dawn shone on us; our heart overflows with gratitude, amazement, premonitions, expectation, – at long last the horizon appears free to us again, even if it should not be bright; at long last our ships may venture out again, venture out to face any danger; all the daring of the lover of knowledge is permitted again; the sea, our sea, lies open again; perhaps there has never yet been such an 'open sea'.

Reality exists uncreated and without point or purpose. It has no historical direction, though Nietzsche considered that if it exists infinitely then there are periodic cycles of recurrence in which events are repeated endlessly (like Sisyphus's ascent and decline). We are on our own, but without the comfort of universal solidarity, for the notions of brotherhood or common humanity are illusions constructed in a wretched effort to hold reality at bay. Nietzsche's arguments against religion are indirect. First, he thought that primitive religious beliefs were based on simple errors about the causes of natural events. Second, in common with many educated Protestants of his generation, he felt that historical criticism had shown scripture to have no authority and precious little credibility. Third, he postulated psychological and social forces that had favoured the development of Christianity. Fourth, and relatedly, he identified widespread motives that Christianity served, these being antithetical to human life as he conceived it.

These are not philosophical refutations of the very possibility of theism, such as the argument from evil aims to be. Nor are they demonstrations of the internal incoherence of Christian doctrines. Rather, Nietzsche is saying that religion was born out of ignorance, nurtured as a reaction to weakness, and kept alive in the interest of the 'herd'. This mode of criticism is also advanced by his admirer Sigmund Freud (1856-1939), most famously in *The Future of an Illusion* (1927), where he analyses religious beliefs as wish-fulfilling deceptions. Finding themselves in a world not of their making, bristling with threats to health, happiness and life itself, human beings fashion images of other possibilities, in particular of an all-powerful father figure controlling the world and providing for our survival into eternity: 'illusions, fulfilments of the oldest, strongest and most urgent wishes of mankind'.

These challenging conjectures may well be contested, but even if they were true they would not show that Christianity is false. Earlier I distinguished between ends conceived of as points of cessation, and as goals. At this point, it is important to mark the difference between reasons as motives and as evidential grounds. Depth (socio)psychology of the sort practised in different ways by Nietzsche, Marx and Freud is interested in tracing motives for actions, but any assessment of the plausibility of religious claims (as contrasted with the psychology of religious claimants) must attend to such premises or reasons as may sustain them. The fact that a belief is held in consequence of hope or fear, and that maintaining it confers advantage or imposes cost, has no immediate bearing on whether it is true or false. Looking to extraneous causes and effects may be relevant if one is interested in the genesis of someone's beliefs. So far as their truth is concerned, however, that must be determined on the basis of direct evaluation. Of course, where one has good reason to believe that a set of beliefs is false, especially if one judges that it is incoherent, then it makes sense to look for other explanations of why it is maintained. No doubt Nietzsche thought that scripture had been shown to be evidentially unreliable (Marx and Freud took it to be conspicuously mythical – symbolic of an imagined human essence, and of neurotic preoccupations, respectively), but that hardly touches the question of the truth of theism *per se*. In addition, the historical criticism that cast doubt on scripture often begged questions against it; by presuming, for example, that reports of miracles were to be dismissed on the grounds that such things cannot happen. Nietzsche's arguments against Christianity presume it to be false (as do those of Marx and Freud). They do not show it to be so.

This said, Nietzsche's criticisms of the moral character of Judaeo-Christianity need to be considered. The two most enduring elements in his overall philosophy are: first, the negative claim that the world, and *a fortiori* each individual life, has no objective meaning; and, second, the positive thesis that meanings are 'made' as human beings propose values to themselves. It is on account of the first that Nietzsche may properly be described as a 'metaphysical nihilist', meaning not that he values nothing but that he believes that, strictly speaking, nothing is of value. It is because of the details of his positive thesis – involving the 'Will to Power' and the ascent of the post-Christian 'Super-man' (*Übermensch*) – that he has come, somewhat unfairly, to be associated with the doctrines of National Socialism. His challenge to religious moralities is twofold: first, that they deceive themselves in supposing that there is an objective order of meanings and values (deriving from God's plan for the world); and second, that the system of values they have arrived at is one fit only for the weak and inferior. Nietzsche claims both to identify the origins of ethical thinking (to offer a 'genealogy of morals'), and to reveal the character of it (to give an analysis of the different kinds of value system).

He distinguishes between 'master' and 'slave' moralities. The former is aristocratic, evaluating characters as 'noble' or 'despicable' depending on whether they demonstrate proper or inadequate concern for the interests of the strong. The latter is the way of the multitude, being concerned with what is to the advantage of the many, who are weak and fearful. Strength and independence are valued by those of aristocratic spirit, and feared by those of slavish heart. Sympathy and kindness are spurned by the strong but craved by the weak. These sets of attitudes constitute contrasting responses to the absence of objective meaning. The higher men are unshaken by the circumstance of a silent and pointless cosmos. The lowly live in dread, deceive themselves, and fashion a morality of absolute, universal requirements by which the spirit of the strong may be tamed and their energies harnessed to the service of the weak. The animating force in this levelling process is resentment (*ressentiment*) arising from the recognition of slavishness. Although Nietzsche thought there were other forms of slave morality, Christianity (with its emphasis on compassion, charity, humility, self-denial and the acceptance of suffering) is the major cultural product of resentment. As such it should be viewed with contempt by the true noble: the man who makes his own values in accord with his own self-determining will. In *The Anti-Christ* (1888), Nietzsche writes: 'Christianity has waged a war to the death against this higher type of man ... [it] has taken the side of everything weak, base, ill-constituted, it has made an ideal out of opposition to the instinct of strong life ... [it] is a revolt of everything that crawls along the ground directed against that which is elevated.' (It should be added that socialism, social democracy, and welfare-liberalism emerge on this account as secular variants of the Christian ethic. Nietzsche is particularly scathing of socialism, seeing it as no more than a reformulation, under pressure of secularisation, of the ongoing effort to enlist the simmering mass of mediocrity in the task of constraining the strong with ties of universal obligation and other-regarding duties.)

In all of this there is much to contest: the idea that charity is to be equated with pity; the insistence that self-denial is slavish; the claim that acceptance of suffering is a suppression of the spirit of life; the contention that Christianity is an expression of resentment; and that religion in general is essentially a matter of conduct not belief. Is it not more plausible to suppose that sympathy, compassion and humility may be true virtues expressing genuine concerns, and not, as Nietzsche insists, motives of vanity in the promotion of the self and malice in the humiliation of others? And why should we not take the utterance of the credal words '*Credo in unum Deum*' ('I believe in one God') to express what the speaker holds true about reality, rather than side with the philosophers of suspicion who see it as a symptom of existential pathology? Indeed, it is tempting to apply something of the Nietzschean methodology to raise the question whether such a strained view of Christian values does not derive from anxiety about the possibility of ever living up to them. I say this not meaning to imply that Nietzsche was peculiarly incapable of meeting the Christian vocation, but only that, like others of us, he may have felt daunted by the scale of the challenge it poses.

Here, however, I am less interested in defending Christianity against Nietzsche's criticisms, and more concerned with the adequacy of his recommended alternative to traditional 'objectivist' understandings of morality. His alternative combines a view of human greatness as open to the few on the basis of their heroic determination to face up to the tragic nature of existence, with an account of 'authentic' value as being the product of creative self-expression. Interestingly, in light of the parallels with Camus, and with Sisyphus as Camus represents him, Nietzsche took pride in his own willingness to embrace the possibility of eternal recurrence, not in a mood of stoic resignation but with a spirit of affirmation, taking it up as more material to be fashioned into a self-created masterwork.

Although the structure of the genealogies, analyses, metaphors and analogies differs, there emerges a common theme of much modern and postmodern thought: that there is no objective meaning, but that one may yet attain some kind of existential warrant by living resolutely in the face of that fact. The claim that this is a satisfactory solution to the search for personal meaning is analogous to one answer to an old philosophical question about the nature of value. Are happiness, friendship, knowledge, justice, liberty, etc. good because we desire them, or do we desire them because they are good? As with all philosophical questions, much ingenuity has been exercised in formulating a range of answers. There is, though, a clear opposition between the idea that something may be valuable independently of whether it is desired, and that what it is for something to have value is just for it to be valued.

The philosophical origins of this latter position lie with the Sophists of Greek antiquity, summarised in the saying of Protagoras (*c*. 490-420 BC) that 'man is the measure [standard] of all things.' Its most influential formulation, however, is David Hume's. In his *Treatise of Human Nature* (1739) Hume claims that there is no matter of fact concerning the goodness or badness of things, beyond the sentiments of approval or disapproval we feel towards them:

> Take any action allow'd to be vicious [evil]: Wilful murder, for instance. Examine it in all lights, and see if you can find that matter of fact, or real existence, which you call vice … The vice entirely escapes you, as long as you consider the object. You never can find it, till you turn your reflexion into your own breast, and find a sentiment of disapprobation, which arises in you, towards this action … It lies in yourself, not in the object … Vice and virtue, therefore … are not qualities in objects but perceptions in the mind.

This is a fine instance of Hume's style: the vivid example of the seemingly obvious, undone by a few simple observations, and the understatement of a thesis which leads to a revolutionary conclusion – the refutation of traditional understandings of morality. There is an issue whether Hume's position is best understood as saying that moral and other value judgments are statements *about* the speaker's own feelings, or that they are expressions *of* those feelings. This need not detain us, for the essential point is the denial of moral objectivity, conjoined with the suggestion that value is something we bestow upon things – including our own lives and human life in general – and not something we discover them to have. Although it lacks the vehemence of Nietzsche's nihilism, and the melancholy of Camus's absurd, Hume's relaxed subjectivism is no less radical from the point of view of the quest for objective value and meaning: for, like them, it maintains that there are no such things.

Hume was consciously opposing the long tradition of moral objectivism found in the writings of Plato, Aristotle, Cicero, Augustine and Aquinas. No doubt because of the influence of these figures, but also because of its plausibility, it is a common presumption that moral judgments may be true or false, and that whether they are one or the other depends on whether they state what is objectively the case. It is also part of moral thinking that fundamental moral claims are universally binding on all competent persons, and that some of these claims are absolute, admitting no exceptions or special cases. Thus, for example, it is commonly supposed that it is always and everywhere wrong, for anyone, whatever their reasons, to torture a human infant or to kill human beings for pleasure. Notwithstanding these examples of the objectivist assumption of common morality, and of the universal and absolute character of some of its requirements, this view has sometimes been challenged by forms of cultural and moral relativism. We live in just such a time.

Typically the challenge arises when an established culture encounters the different religious beliefs, moral values and associated practices of other societies. It was just such discoveries by the Greeks that contributed to the rise of Sophistic relativism. In his *Histories* (*c.* 440 BC), Herodotus observes that people take their own religions and customs to be correct, and that there are seemingly very different beliefs and codes in different cultures. He tells of how Darius, king of Persia, summoned some Greeks and asked what he would have to pay to get them to eat their fathers when they died. They replied that nothing would compensate for doing such a terrible thing. Then, with the Greeks still present, he called in Indians of the Callatiae tribe whose custom was to eat their fathers, and asked what he would have to give for the Callatians to burn them instead (as was Greek practice). The Indians were horrified, and urged him not even to mention such an abomination. The point of cultural difference could hardly have been lost on Darius's hearers, or on Herodotus's readers.

Along with moral disagreement *within* a society, as represented now by the disputes in Britain, the United States and other countries over such issues as homosexuality, human cloning, abortion, and euthanasia, marked disagreement *between* cultures is taken by relativists to provide support for their particular brand of moral subjectivism. An example of this position, apt because it returns us to the attacks of 11 September, is provided in a recent article by the prominent American literary theorist Stanley Fish. (Entitled 'Don't Blame Relativism', it was published as part of a symposium styled 'Can Postmodernists Condemn Terrorism?' in *The Responsive Community*, Summer 2002.) Beginning with the sentence 'Are you now or have you ever been a postmodernist?' Fish hints at the possibility of a McCarthy-like witch-hunt. He goes on to develop the worry that postmodernists (such as himself) will be scapegoated for the events, because of their denial that there are universal moral absolutes by which the attacks may be judged and condemned, and for holding instead that 'there is more than one way to see the crisis'. His response is to claim that postmodernist relativism actually presents the solution to the question of how we may judge the Islamic terrorists, and not a denial that we are entitled to do so. This is because it saves moral judgment from the vacuity of absolutist objectivism:

At times like these, all nations fall back on, and are right to fall back on, the record of aspiration and accomplishment that makes up their citizens' understanding of what they live by and for. That understanding is sufficient, and far from undermining its sufficiency, postmodern thought underwrites it by sending us back to the justificatory grounds we rely on in ordinary life after having turned us away from the illusory justification of universal absolutes to which every party subscribes but all define differently.

This is rhetorically agile but intellectually unsatisfactory. First, it fails to engage the question of how moral values can be distinguished from social conventions such as etiquette. Second, it provides no credible means of arbitration between competing value systems, and so leaves inter- and intra-cultural criticism open to the charge of being no more than the assertion of one set of commitments or sentiments against another. Third, it is self-serving in its characterisation of the possibilities of justification: implying that the remaining opposition is between an empty absolutism and the most radical personal subjectivism, so allowing postmodernism to appear a moderate position. Fourth, it characterises the justifications provided by the latter in reassuring terms that more properly belong to traditional moral thought. The last is an almost Humean flourish.

For Fish the disagreement between Islamic terrorists and the citizens of the US is like the difference between the Greeks and the Callatians. Each has their set of apparently conflicting ideologies and values, and each criticises the behaviour of the other. But whereas a traditional moral objectivist maintains that beyond these commitments lie the moral realities of the case, and that these (and not feelings of approval or disapproval) determine the correct judgment; the postmodernist holds that each sides' views are only rooted in 'the record of aspiration and accomplishment that makes up their citizens' understanding of what they live by and for'. I say 'only' because while such a record *might* reflect the recognition of objective values, the postmodernist says it never does. For him, moral right and wrong, like existential meaning and meta-narratives, are projected inventions.

It is not enough, of course, to show that the styles of invention and projection implied by the views of Hume, Nietzsche, Camus and Fish fail to deliver meaning and value as these are ordinarily understood, for it is precisely their view that this ordinary understanding is illusory. That it is so is held to be revealed by the fact of disagreement, and that it must be so is taken to follow from the impossibility of providing objectivist accounts of morality, personal meaning or world history. Let me address these points in turn. With regard to ethical disagreement it is first necessary to distinguish its different varieties. Workers may find themselves in dispute with an employer over whether their wages are *just*. One side claims they are; the other denies this. A hospital committee may be divided over whether to permit certain medical experiments involving infant or geriatric patients. Some members say the lack of consent prohibits it on grounds of *dignity* and *inviolability*; others dispute this. Evidently in such cases the disagreement is not over whether values are objective, and nor is it over whether justice, dignity, and inviolability are values to be respected. They concern instead the difficulties of applying these concepts in the complex circumstances of life, in which the protection or promotion of other values is also at issue. There is nothing here to show that values are invented. Quite the contrary.

A second kind of disagreement is that recorded by Herodotus, concerning divergence between the moral and religious views held in different societies. The Greeks saw the cremation of one's dead father as an act of pious respect, but viewed the prospect of eating the corpse as vile. The Callatians regarded the first as an abomination, and the second to be right and fitting. First-world medical associations generally oppose the policy of even voluntary euthanasia. Several third-world peoples practise it. In *Purity and Danger* (1966), Mary Douglas reports how the Nuer of Sudan disposed of deformed infants by putting them by the river in the area of hippopotami, who the Nuer believed were their real fathers. Similar contrasts can be found by comparing cultures at different stages in their histories. The Nuer beliefs and practices have European analogues in the treatment of malformed babies as 'changelings'. It was believed that elves and goblins swapped their inferior offspring for human children, and that some changelings had been fathered by demons. Martin Luther (1483-1546) held that changelings are substituted by Satan in order to plague and trouble mankind. He even records meeting a changeling in 1532 at Dessau and saying to the Elector of Saxony that if he (Luther) were ruler he would 'throw this child into the water and dare commit homicide on him'. It should go without saying that any present-day Lutheran would take a very different view.

Once again, however, these disagreements lend no support to the relativist position. For the examples are not cases of the same action or policy being judged right according to one set of values and wrong relative to another. What the Greeks condemned is impiety in the treatment of the dead, and the Callatians did likewise. Their differences concern whether eating or burning the dead are necessarily disrespectful, or whether they might not be different ways of expressing piety. Similarly, the behaviour of the Nuer, and the attitudes of Luther with regard to deformed children, are quite different from what would generally be regarded as infanticide. For whereas we believe that the poor creatures are human beings to be treated with care and respect, the Nuer believed them to be semi-human; and Luther regarded the Dessau changeling as non-human, 'only a piece of flesh' (*massa carnis*). What these and the earlier disagreements actually point to is the existence of commonly recognised human values; the pursuit of which has to take account of conceptual issues (working out whether a practice or policy is in accord with them), as well as empirical matters (determining the natures of things).

At one point in his *Philosophical Investigations* (1951), Wittgenstein asks how, if you arrived in a strange country where people speak an unfamiliar language, you would begin to work out what they were saying. His answer is that 'the common behaviour of mankind is the system of reference by means of which we interpret an unknown language.' In other words, within cultural diversity lies a common humanity. Indeed, just as the great variety of dishes at a multi-ethnic food festival is to be understood in terms of universal human needs and interests, so social and cultural diversity can only be made sense of against a background of presumed human commonality. This also provides the key to understanding the nature of value and shows what is wrong with Hume's claim that good and bad are not observable as matters of fact.

If something is not made good by our desiring it, why then should its being good give us reason to desire it? Consider the values I listed earlier – happiness, friendship, knowledge, justice, liberty. What makes these good? The ancient and still compelling answer is that they are constituent elements of human flourishing. People are happy in so far as they enjoy various conditions in their lives. Those conditions are contributed to, or consist in the experience of genuine friendship, the attainment of significant knowledge, the presence or exercise of justice and liberty, and so on. More generally, an action or policy is good (and, *pace* Hume, can be discovered to be such) to the extent that it promotes or instantiates some part of the good of those involved; and that it is bad if it inhibits or destroys that good.

So far as that good itself is concerned, its content is given by the nature of the being in question. Plants need nutrients, heat and light. Without some level of these they cannot live well (or at all), but given these and other favourable conditions they may flourish. A good life for a cat consists in the full development and unimpeded exercise of those powers that constitute cat life: powers of nutrition, sensation, motion, association, reproduction and so on. The same holds true for a human being in so far as he or she is an animal possessed of similar biological functions. But human nature goes beyond these powers to include the complexity of an emotional, aesthetic, intellectual, deliberative, and extensively social being. At this point we can see at least one way in which religion comes into the picture of the human good. Pagan Roman writers and early Christian fathers speculated on the origins of the term 'religion' (*religio*). Cicero conjectured that it derives from *relegere* (to treat carefully) and arose because of the care taken in rituals. The more plausible account, however, is that originating with Lactantius (4th century), who relates it to the verb *religare* (to bind), saying that it is from men's being 'tied' to God by the bond of piety that religion got its name. Although Lactantius was a Christian, the account is intended to be general. In other words, the idea of religion arises naturally in the minds of rational creatures as they find themselves in a world not of their making, speculate about the order, origin and possible governance of nature, and feel bound by piety towards that transcendent source. If being human involves being disposed towards reality in this manner, then the cultivation of a proper 'religious' sensibility, like the cultivation of an aesthetic one, is a part of the human good.

Consider again the nature of value as I have presented it. Goodness is to be understood in terms of the flourishing of life. Life, however, is an ordered integration of a whole series of functions and purposes co-operating for the good of the whole. The same unity-towards-fulfilment is characteristic of the higher powers in a rationally well-ordered existence. But we can ask what this is directed towards. In the course of a day, an individual's activities and experiences may stand in isolation or disarray, or they may have meaning as parts of larger value-promoting projects. Likewise, the actions of one may stand alone, or they may be part of a co-operative social project, perhaps a transgenerational one. Now a series of hierarchies of activities within and between lives can be seen to emerge; these being given unity and value, at each stage, by the ends towards which they are directed.

In summary: given, first, the refutation of the negative claims of value-nihilism; second, the demonstration of the inadequacy of their subjectivist alternatives; and third, the provision of a positive account of value as involving the development and exercise of the powers proper to the nature of a being, I conclude, echoing the ending of the previous chapter, that the objectivity of morality is best secured by an understanding which sees human existence as aimed towards a transcendent goal. If that is right, then the course of each human life, and of our lives together, is a religious one – a movement towards or away from God. To this may be added the considerations of chapter 2, that the very idea of purpose calls out for an explanation in terms of design. There is one sense, certainly, in which we may be 'authors' of our own lives; but as we fashion our existence this way or that, we do so using our natural functions and powers which we may command but which we did not create. The very possibility of pursuing an objectively meaningful life depends, therefore, both on a goal transcendent of those we may happen to propose to ourselves, and on the prior organisation of nature, especially our own nature. This provides at least one interpretation of the old idea that God is both the beginning and the end of things: their source and their completion. As Tolstoy (1817-75) puts it in *My Confession* (1905), recording his own struggle with the question of life's significance: 'in faith alone could we find the meaning and possibility of life.' Quite how our lives may be completed *in* God is an issue to which I shall return.

6

Religion, Art and the Aesthetic

The hard rind of nature and the common world give the mind more trouble in breaking through to the Absolute than do the products of art.

G.W.F. Hegel

The idea that value pertains to the natures of things, especially in the exercise of their proper powers, reinforces the earlier explanation of evil as the privation or lack of what is required for proper function and, *a fortiori*, for flourishing. This also provides for a distinctive account of the character of beauty as it is encountered in the experience of nature and in the making of art. In this chapter I shall explore the relevance of these matters to the reasonableness of religion. My claims may be sum-marised briefly by saying first, that the experience of the aesthetic may warrant religious beliefs; and, second, that the practice of art-making is best understood as a mode of religious expression. These two ideas evidently stand in opposition to a common humanistic conception of art and the aesthetic as alternative sources of interpretation, consolation and sustenance for those for whom theism is unbelievable.

First, then, it is a familiar thought that natural beauty may offer an intimation of creation. Indeed, for many people now detached from traditional religious creeds and practices, the experience of nature may provide the best prospect of any sense of transcendence. The impact of Darwin's *Origin of Species* and of other secular theories on the religious faith of educated Victorians was a matter of concern to Matthew Arnold (1822-88). In 'The Study of Poetry' (1888), Arnold remarked that 'More and more mankind will discover that we have to turn to poetry to interpret life for us, to console us, to sustain us ... and most of what now passes with us for religion and philosophy will be replaced by poetry.' The implied assessment of the future of religion is reflected in the melancholy of his own famous poem 'Dover Beach' (1867):

> The sea of faith
> Was once, too, at the full, and round Earth's shore
> Lay like the folds of a bright girdle furl'd;
> But now I only hear
> Its melancholy, long, withdrawing roar,
> Retreating, to the breath
> Of the night-wind, down the vast edges drear
> And naked shingles of the world.

It is ironic that nature should have provided Arnold with an image of his age's loss of faith, for in the minds of contemporaries it was precisely the experience of nature that offered a way back to the idea of creation. In *The*

6. RELIGION, ART AND THE AESTHETIC

Purple Land (1885), a novel about Uruguay, W.H. Hudson (1841-1922) has a character observe how amid the natural beauties of that country 'the religion that languishes in crowded cities or steals shame-faced to hide itself in dim churches, flourishes greatly, filling the soul with a solemn joy. Face to face with Nature on the vast hills at eventide, who does not feel himself near to the Unseen?' And just about midway between these writings by Arnold and Hudson, Gerard Manley Hopkins (1844-89) wrote 'God's Grandeur' (1877), which gives renewed vigour to the old claim that nature shows the presence of God, while also explaining why, in a heavily industrialised and crowded Victorian England, this was less evident than in quieter, more pastoral times:

> The world is charged with the grandeur of God.
> It will flame out, like shining from shook foil;
> It gathers to a greatness, like the ooze of oil
> Crushed. Why do men then now not reck his rod?
> Generations have trod, have trod, have trod;
> And all is seared with trade; bleared, smeared with toil;
> And wears man's smudge and shares man's smell: the soil
> Is bare now, nor can foot feel, being shod.

A second point of relevance, illustrated by these lines, is that the aesthetic experience of nature has often provided inspiration for the making of works expressing attitudes of 'natural religion': that is to say, the crafting of responses to the sense of the world as significant of something transcendent. This sense of the world as created may take two forms, corresponding in broad terms to the cosmological and teleological arguments discussed in chapter 2.

To begin with, there is the sense of awe at the very being of the world. Here individual things serve to mediate, through their derivative participation in it, a sense of Being itself. This may be induced by attention to things large or small, natural or human or animal made. It can just as easily be triggered by attending to a glass or a piece of thread, as to a mountain range or to the night sky, but the primordiality, scale and permanence of the latter place them among the primary objects of this existential gaze. The still lifes of artists of everyday contemplation such as Chardin (1699-1779) and Morandi (1890-1964) show, however, that this sense of existential significance is available at every turn if one simply sits and gazes.

There is also the sense of manifest design felt in observing the beauty of organisms whose parts stand in fitting relation to one another and to the life of the whole. More profound than the experience of pleasing effects, such as clouds stretched across the sky at sunset, curling plumes of smoke, or the reflection of moonlight on waves, is the recognition of the beauty of natural forms. When we judge the appearance of a human or animal face or body, when we appreciate the visible organisation of a plant, noting the spiralling of the leaf growth, the architectural structure of veins and fibres and so on, we judge beauty relative to the nature of the thing in question. In the *Summa Theologiae*, Aquinas writes that three things are required for beauty: *integrity*, *proportion* and *clarity*. What he means is that we judge something beautiful when it has the parts appropriate to a thing of that sort, when these stand in their proper relations, and when this formal good order is apparent. This provides further confirmation of the idea that value pertains to the natures of things, with the explanation of evil as privation now serving as an account of ugliness.

A third consideration is that just as the experience of nature has led some to a belief in God, so has the experience of art: both art in general, as testifying again to the significance of beauty, and religious art in particular, as presenting aspects of the transcendent. This leads to a fourth point, namely that within particular religious traditions the arts have had an important role in focusing the minds of the faithful on the deity, and in shaping the forms through which the divine is approached in adoration or worship.

Quoting the poet and philosopher Friedrich Schiller, Max Weber famously wrote of 'the disenchantment of the world' effected by the rise of modern science in the post-medieval period. Part of that disenchantment came with the substitution of quantity for quality as the marker of significant difference. For the ancients and the medievals, things were the loci of natures and essences, and even places and times might carry their own significant identities, as in the contrast between sacred and secular in relation to spaces, hours and seasons. Of each thing one might ask *quid est*? (what is it?) and hope to have this answered by a specification of its *quiddity* (its what-it-is-ness). This pre-modern view also included the idea explored in the previous chapter, that nature is dynamic and purposeful. Thus, to understand the *quiddity* of an object was to see it as an agent in process of realising its nature. That small dark, shiny oval which is *actually* a seed is *potentially* a tree; containing within itself the plan of its own development. If you do not understand that, you do not know what the thing is, even if you know the mass, position and velocity of every particle it contains. An egg is not just a quantity of viscous liquid, but the instantiation of a specific essence on course to being a bird. A human embryo is not just a mass of matter or even a sack of cells, but a human being in progress to maturity and adulthood. So, too, with collections of objects linked by common natures or natural bonds. The life of an individual bird may be tied to that of a migrating flock. Whole ranges of flora and fauna may be bound together in micro-environments and those within larger 'eco-systems'. In each case, things are seen to involve the dynamic unfolding of natures. Thus for the medievals the central descriptive and explanatory idea was that of the 'substantial form' of a thing (*forma rei*) as revealed through its activities. It is this that is also the focus of the second, more profound form of experience of beauty in nature.

In time, however, medieval Aristotelianism gave way to Galileo's mechanical system, to Descartes' geometry of volumes, and to the sciences of measurement. In obvious ways innovatory, this change also represented a return to the old philosophy of the Greek atomists for whom all things are merely aggregations of particles in the void, and all qualitative differences effects of quantitative and combinatory variation. In his *Principles of Philosophy* (1644), Descartes (1596-1650) acknowledges the proximity of his view to that of the atomists, and summarises his own central ideas:

> I had observed that nothing at all belonged to the nature of essence of body save that it was a thing with length and breadth and depth, admitting of various shapes and various movements ... in no way do we apprehend in [these] external objects, that which we call light, colour, smell, taste, sound, heat or cold, and the other tactile qualities, or that which we call their substantial forms.

This is close to what Hume was to say a century later. There is, however, an important difference: whereas Descartes believed that what he had observed still served to prove the existence of God and of the soul, Hume believed that neither of these metaphysical entities is intimated, and that neither has to be posited. In his last work, *The Crisis of European Sciences* (1938), Edmund Husserl (1859-1938), the Austrian philosopher and founder of phenomenology, caught this change when he wrote of the influence of Galileo and of Descartes in promoting 'the mathematisation of nature' and of the resulting 'technisation' (*technisierung*) of that mathematical representation in increasingly abstract, formal analyses. In a section headed 'The Life-World as the Forgotten Meaning-Fundament of Natural Science', Husserl writes: 'we must note something of the highest importance that occurred even as early as Galileo: the surreptitious substitution of the mathematically substructured world of idealities for the only real world, the one that is actually given through perception, that is ever experienced and experienceable – our everyday life-world (*lebenswelt*).'

The world mathematised and disenchanted still offers something to the artistic imagination, but the art inspired by this style of austerely pared-down scientific description is, of necessity, silent on the very things that animate ordinary experience. Not only does the scientific account eschew talk of colour, smell, taste, sound and so on, it does not deign to speak of the sense of self and of other, of love and of loss, of memory and of anticipation. Seen from the perspective of the atoms and of their smaller constituents, these qualities and states are transient wisps, vaporous by-products of particles in motion. Similarly, the quiddities of the medievals are eliminated by this account. Whatever the truth concerning the relationship between matter and mind, however, it is mind that matters. So far as purpose, meaning and value are concerned, there is an intimate relationship between the facts and ordinary experience. The microphysical may lie far out of sight and deep below the level of animation, but the realities of birth and death, growth and decay, hunger and satisfaction, despair and joy, experienced harmony and felt discord all remain part of the real world given in and through perception.

Any art that aims to make sense of these vital features must therefore necessarily be 'phenomenological', an aesthetic exploration of felt qualitative differences, and of perceived significance. This is not to say that it is *only* a description of the surfaces of things. Like the philosopher and the natural scientist, the artist is, or should be, interested in making some sense of the unapparent, and of probing appearances to determine whether reality stops with them, or whether it extends further into areas that cannot be experienced or even adequately conceived. The idea that it might do this may be anathema to someone whose business is always to conceptualise a given subject matter. Notwithstanding the aspirations of some artists to be 'conceptualists', however, the fact is that art is ultimately a practical and not a speculative mode of knowledge. Artists, of all people, should be alive to the possibility that where *saying* has run out there may still be *showing*; and even, to speak paradoxically, alive to the possibility of making visible what cannot be seen, tangible what cannot be felt, and audible what cannot be heard.

In his *Sonnets to Orpheus* (1917), Rilke (1875-1926) honours the Greek demigod of music whose playing and singing were so entrancingly beautiful that animals and even trees and stones were drawn to listen to him. The words of Sonnet 10 of Part 2 are singularly apt to the present context:

But for us, existence is still enchanted;
still in a hundred places the source. A play of pure powers,
touched only by those who kneel and wonder.
Words still go softly forth in the unsayable ...
And music, ever new, from trembling stones,
builds her divine home in useless space.

The impulse to fashion not only what is practically useful but what has significant meaning lies deep in humankind. One of the longest chapters of the book of Confucian wisdom known as the *Liki* is devoted to the origins, meaning and value of music. In it Confucius (551-479 BC) makes a series of comparisons between music and ritual which he regards as complementary aspects of a spiritual response to the world. He observes that 'music rises from the human heart: when the emotions are touched by the external world ... Music expresses the harmony of the universe while rituals express its order.' The earliest musical notes made by men were, perhaps, part of some stone age percussion, tapped out with clicking stones. Somewhat later, bone whistles, shells and animal horns served as wind instruments. Most likely these were played before or after the hunt, perhaps in early rituals of petition or thanksgiving. Whether these were the origins of sacred music remains speculative. It is a fact, however, that the earliest known examples of musical notation are a set of Phoenician clay fragments (*c.* 1200 BC) that appear to record a hymn to Nikkal, a moon goddess. Living in the same general area during the following centuries, the writers of Hebrew scripture made further links between music and religion. In the book of Samuel and in the Second Book of Kings, for example, it is reported that bands of prophets played instruments in order that they might be possessed of the spirit of God. The Christian church of the Apostolic period comprised Jewish and other Near-Eastern converts. Something of the music of the Phoenicians and of the Hebrews may survive, therefore, in Christian liturgies: both in Eastern Catholic rite and orthodox hymns, and in the Gregorian chant of the Western Church, which draws remotely on the Hebrew cantor's recitation of the psalms. Certainly there is in these cases, as there was no doubt in the hymn composed in honour of the goddess Nikkal, and even perhaps in the bellow of the horns and the trembling stones assembled by the stone age performers, an encouragement to kneel and wonder in the presence of pure forces in an enchanted world.

If it is likely that the first notes humans ever played were made in emulation of the sounds of animals, it is almost certain that the first things humans ever painted were themselves. The earliest known evidence of pigments being ground for use in decoration comes from a cave near Lusaka in Zambia. These powdery deposits appear to be more than 300,000 years old, and they come from a part of world generally presumed to be the area of the origination of *homo sapiens*, though they predate the emergence of modern man. The purpose for which they were prepared is unknown, but there are no fragments of decorated artefacts, and given what can be surmised of the lives of these earliest pigment grinders, and what is known of other early cave dwellers, it is presumed that they decorated themselves for hunting rituals or other ceremonies. Much better known in the prehistory of art are the cave paintings in France and Spain, which are 30-35,000 years old. These include unmistakable images of the hunt, typically showing great beasts on the run. The function of the images appears to be that of pictorial narratives, or perhaps that of visual illustrations of practices otherwise described around the fire. In either event, the skill cultivated, the time spent, and the effort taken in producing these images suggests that they were important in the lives of those who made and those who viewed them.

So far as sculpture is concerned, the earliest conspicuously representative pieces are fertility figures dating from 20,000 or more years ago. Carved in the round, the originals of these large-breasted, swollen-stomached and often faceless creatures, such as the Venus of Willendorf or the later Mediterranean 'fat ladies', are evidently not portraits. Again they signify general conditions critical to the processes of human life, and were probably objects of veneration or instruments of magic. Long before men learned to carve or to make pictorial representations, however, they may have turned their efforts beyond body painting to the making of autonomous aesthetic objects. Again the evidence comes from the protection of an African cave, this time on the coast of the Southern Cape, and from a period of 70,000 or more years ago. In 2000, archaeologists working in the area found thousands of small pieces of ochre, many of which were rubbed smooth, probably from having been being ground to make pigment. Among these fragments were two pieces of red ochre along whose length parallel lines had been inscribed, with further cross-hatching creating a pattern of diamonds and triangles. These regular shapes, and their appearance on separate stones, provide evidence of a process of abstraction: extracting patterns from the detail of perception, retaining a sense of these and then repeating them carefully.

This double capacity – to fashion the idea of abstracted forms, and then to gather materials for the purpose of recording them in a relatively permanent and highly tactile medium – indicates the appearance of powers of reflection and deliberation. It also marks the emergence of an aesthetic sensibility, which, however primitive, suggests the beginnings of art as a non-utilitarian endeavour: the making of 'useless' things. The course of development between this remote beginning and the art of civilisations such as those of the Far and Near East, the Mediterranean and Northern Europe is evidently a long one, but there remains great potency in the minimal crafting of simple materials. If we want to understand why that should be so, then we need to think of the kind of creativity that is associated with art making and the ways in which it connects with religious ideas.

There are three fundamental kinds of making: *creation*, *generation*, and *modification*. The theistic God of Judaism, Christianity and Islam is a creator in the

strictest sense: he brings things into being not by transforming existing materials, but by willing them into
existence, quite literally out of nothing (*ex nihilo*).
Generation, by contrast, involves the coming to be of one
thing from another. While something genuinely new
exists, there is something prior to it from which it derives
its matter or its form, or both. Although a process of
modification may be extensive, it is the least radical kind
of making, in as much as no new thing comes into existence. Through a process of biological reproduction a tree
is naturally generated. In felling the tree and fashioning a
table from it one (artificially) generates a piece of furniture. In later cutting the legs of the table to lower its top,
one modifies the furniture. Prior to all of this, if the theist
is right, stands God who created *ex nihilo* the matter that
was eventually to become the tree. While human art-
making is clearly not a matter of strict creation, it is more
properly conceived of as generation than as modification
(though it involves modification as well).

When a sculptor carves or constructs an object, what
pre-existed is converted into something new. What was
mere mass becomes articulated volume carrying an
aesthetic charge. When music is composed, sounds are
transformed into an ordered dynamic unity. All at once a
new type of creature is in flight in the world, one in
whose rising and falling we can detect a type of animation. In dance, locomotion becomes gestural. In poetry, a
new kind of meaning is drawn out from spoken and
written words. These transformations and conversions

are also analogically creative in that the kinds of changes they involve are often so radically discontinuous with what previously existed that it makes sense to say that something wholly new has come into being.

This account also provides the key to understanding the idea of the artist as a kind of miracle-worker, if not a quasi-deity. Admittedly, he can only work with what is already in being, but while he may not literally create a world he nevertheless can add to it. Moreover, the logic of art-making is importantly different from that of scientific activity. A physicist or chemist works with known properties of matter to predict effects of their interaction. Sometimes it is largely unknown what the upshot of an experiment may be, and sometimes the result is other than what is predicted. But results are then fed into the theory and subsequent predictions take account of them. In other words the processes under study are presumed to be generally deterministic and wholly empirical. In the case of art-making, by contrast, the production of effects is never a matter of mere linear combination (lines and stacks of stones notwithstanding), and the aesthetic content may go beyond what is given immediately to the senses. The aggregation of matter and the multiplication or complexification of material properties are insufficient of themselves to establish aesthetic significance.

What is being sought is always something emergent, a new kind of reality that resides in the material but is not reducible to it. No physical or chemical theory could predict that physical entities of such and such a sort, in such and such an arrangement, would have meaning or beauty. One might reply that if a work of art were materially replicated then the duplicate would have to be of the same aesthetic value as the original. But that is not a scientific prediction projected up from a knowledge of the material base. Instead it is a philosophical thesis based on the assumption that the material properties are sufficient for the aesthetic ones. It is also false, for among the aspects of a work that we rightly value are such factors as originality, craftsmanship and authenticity and these are missing in the case of the replica.

The fact that matter alone does not make art has encouraged some idealist thinkers in both Eastern and Western traditions to say that, properly speaking, art remains where it is conceived: in the mind. What we see or hear are its effects, like smoke rising from an unseen fire, or echoes repeating long after the event that caused them. On this account the viewer or listener has to re-create the source in his or her own imagination; trying to recover something of the artist's intellectual intuition. Such views enjoy periodic favour among theorists and philosophically-minded artists. In antiquity an intellectualist version is found in Plato; in the Renaissance it was fashionable among members of the Florentine Academy; and in the 18th and 19th centuries an affective version features in the writings of British and Continental European Romantics. Thus, in the preface to the *Lyrical Ballads* (1801), Wordsworth (1770-1850) famously describes poetry as 'the spontaneous overflow of powerful feelings: it takes its origin from emotion recollected in tranquillity.' More recently, in a founding text of conceptualism, *Paragraphs on Conceptual Art* (1967), the American Sol Lewitt describes 'conceptual art' as follows:

> [It] is not theoretical or illustrative of theories [but] intuitive, it is involved with all kinds of mental processes and it is purposeless ... Ideas are discovered by intuition ... the idea itself, even if not made visual, is as much a work of art as any finished product ... the danger is, I think, of making the physicality of the materials so important that it becomes the idea of the work.

The concern not to allow its embodiment to overflow the idea of a work is understandable, but it is wrong to infer that since the matter of an artwork may be distinguishable from its meaning, therefore the two are separable. Two pairs of ideas need to be grasped. First, those of *matter* and *form*, and second, those of *form* and *content*. The form of a tree or of a table – the arrangement of its parts and the functions associated with these – are describable independently of talk about its particular matter. It does not follow, however, that the tree or the table is really some ideal mental entity of which the objects in question are just effects. Rather, the form is realised in, and is not detachable from the wood which embodies it. Form and matter are inseparable and constitute a single reality. Likewise, from the fact that one may describe something of the content of an artwork apart from describing the embodied form of the piece, it does not follow that they are distinct.

The San Sepolcro *Resurrection* (*c.* 1458) by Piero della Francesca (1420-92) shows a group of five figures in a triangular grouping. There are the four sleeping guards grouped between the base line and the parallel formed by the upper edge of the tomb; and the figure of Christ standing upright, his head reaching the apex and his left foot resting on the edge of the sarcophagus. Christ divides the landscape: beyond his raised right arm and the standard held triumphant in it, the scene is of the depths of winter; while to his left the trees are thick with new growth. While Christ is stepping out of the tomb, its shape and form are like an altar on which in later times the offertory of the Mass might be enacted. Since his initial movement is upward, he may also be seen to be stepping onto that altar, as a willing sacrifice, to be followed then by a further ascent into Heaven. The sleeping soldiers represent dormant humanity, like them oblivious to the moment of cosmic salvation. The articulation of the picture plane involves oppositions and reinforcements of colour and texture and the interplay of rigid and fluid contours: the iconic crossing of horizontal (tomb) and vertical (lance) contrasting with the complex swirl of lines and shapes below (the forms of the sleeping guards); these in turn contrasting with the simple sweeping contour of Christ and the undulating form of the horizon partitioning earth and sky.

Applying the categories of form and content one might say that the geometrical and other compositional features constitute the form of the painting, and the depicted resurrection event its content. Given that analysis, one could go on to suggest that the work is more or less similar in form and/or content to others, that it is, for example, identical in religious content to many Renaissance paintings, and closely similar in pictorial form to the *Resurrection* (1457) by Castagno in San Apollonia in Florence. But the analysis and its application fail to capture the sense in which form and content are united. Besides building materially from below, paintings are constructed conceptually from above. What patches of colour or a line amount to in the context of a painting depend on the forms they serve to realize, and what these forms amount to depends on the wider compositional context, and what that achieves depends on the expressive power of the work, and that in turn is partly fixed by the religious conception of the event with which the artist and viewer are working – a conception that is most fully articulated in the painting itself and in an informed and sympathetic response to it. While we may speak of differences and similarities of form and content, as if these were independent variables, the truth is that at the level of descriptive detail and aesthetic response they are inseparable.

There is a similar continuity between description, interpretation and evaluation. Evidently, an artist may accept a commission to produce a work representing something in which he either does not believe or has no interest. We might think of this situation as being like that of someone who writes a sentence he supposes to be false. In general one cannot tell from looking at a sentence whether the writer believes what it says, or even whether he or she understands it. But the relationship between artist, work and audience is different because of the internal connections between content, meaning, value and truth. Familiar charges brought against artists on the basis of their work include complaints of inauthenticity, of discernible lack of conviction, of confused conception, of lack of imagination, of interpretative superficiality, of mere illustration and so on. Such charges are based on looking at works themselves and discerning what is manifest in them.

These several points – about matter, form, content, description, interpretation and evaluation – apply as much to music and the performing arts as to painting, sculpture and literature. *Ave Verum Corpus* ('Hail, the true Body') is a hymn to the Blessed Sacrament saluting the elevated host at the point of its consecration. Its earliest text is attributed to Pope Innocent VI (1282-1362). Innocent does not feature much in Papal histories but this hymn has endured and been the subject of considerable artistic as well as devotional interest. Its three most distinguished musical settings are by William Byrd (1543-1623), Mozart (1756-91) and Edward Elgar (1857-1934). Byrd wrote his setting when he was 62, at a point when hope for a Catholic restoration in England had lapsed, leaving only a longing for the past. In spite of, or perhaps because of this, Byrd's setting is strongly Catholic in character. The richly woven polyphonic texture emphasises the collective worship of the Mass. The waves of sound rising and falling are at once well-delineated and free-floating, as if echoing the mysteries of incarnation and transubstantiation: God become flesh, bread become God. There is also a straining towards the familiar figure of Jesus marked by the rising 'O Jesu fili Mariae' ('Oh Jesus son of Mary'), as if seeking the human figure in the sacramental presence.

Mozart's dealings with religious themes came to be complicated by his interest in Freemasonry and its profession of an undoctrinal form of Christianity, together with its claim to provide access to esoteric knowledge encoded in significant numbers and geometrical figures. His setting of the *Ave Verum* is sensuous and beautifully balanced, but it is more a matter of brilliantly crafted music brought in procession before the throne of Heaven than a direct theological engagement with the idea that the resurrected flesh of Christ has come to replace the mundane element of bread. Elgar represents a return to informed orthodoxy, but while his strong repeated melody floats heavenward like rising incense it still stands at some remove from the subject of the hymn. As with Mozart the music seems more self-contained, soothing and comforting than befits the proper religious focus of the hymn.

When an artist seriously and committedly develops a theme or idea, what he or she produces stands as a presentation of the reality and values in which the work seeks to participate. The guiding idea is a starting point, but its full articulation is the work itself. One should, therefore, think of a painting or musical composition not as an effect of an artistic conception, but as that conception in material form. Whether the work is an elementary response to the experience of the world as a place of powers and spirits, a more complex engagement with the idea of natural order and purpose, a meditation on the sacred meaning of history, or a presentation of religious dogma, in judging it we are judging the credibility of what it proclaims. One implication of this is that art of religious or moral significance is aesthetically worse for being false in these respects. By the same token, we cannot separate a favourable aesthetic evaluation from a judgment as to the truth of what it presents. If we arrive at the former then we have to that extent embraced the latter. The present significance of this should be apparent, for much of the great art of the world is religious in one or more of its source, purpose and content. That may trouble atheists who would rather art dealt with realities as they understand them, but they might have comforted themselves with the thought that the appreciation of religious art as art poses no challenge to non-belief. That, however, is what I am contesting. A serious favourable appreciation of the aesthetic value of a work of art carries an implication of acceptance of its content as constituting a consideration in favour of what is presented. Such are the interconnections between description, interpretation and evaluation, that finding good is in a sense finding credible and to an extent finding true. Those inclined to dismiss this should set themselves the task of giving an illuminating and convincing account of the aesthetic merit of a work of religious art in terms that are altogether neutral as regards the truth and spiritual value of its content.

In thinking about religious art it is natural to consider great works associated with particular faiths, and this poses the challenge that since religions differ in doctrine it is impossible that a favourable assessment of religiously diverse works implies acceptance of what they present. That overlooks two points. First, different religions tend to share beliefs in a transcendent reality, a creative mindful cause, and so on, and it is often these ideas that constitute the essential content of religious art, whether they are expressed in general forms or in relation to faith-specific narratives. Second, from the fact that one faith does not advance the particular claims of another it does not follow that what is proclaimed by artworks relating to each contradicts claims made by the others. And where they do conflict the implication of my argument is that aesthetic evaluation is relevant to determining where religious truth lies. Intelligent persons should not rest content with the sort of superficial aesthetic assessment that fails to take account of truth and falsity; and the reward of a deeper evaluation of religious art is an insight into religious truth.

Some art stands on the edge of being religious, some is imprecisely so, and some is highly specific in doctrinal content. The art of Piero della Francesca or of William

Byrd stand towards the latter end of the spectrum; the prehistoric examples lie at the former end. When describing the carved pieces of red ochre I observed that they tell us things about the mind and sensibility of their maker. So it is more generally, for activity expresses nature. It also serves, however, to develop and transform it. The alchemists sought to turn base metal into gold, but this was only half of their ambition. The material transformation was believed to parallel a conversion of the alchemist himself from mortal flesh into eternal spirit. Art aims at something similar: to transform matter into meaning, and to raise up the spirit of the maker. In some religious traditions art-making is an avowedly sacred practice; but even where someone may be working with only a vague conception of transformation he or she may yet achieve intimations of transcendence.

In the late 1990s the Indian-born British artist Anish Kapoor made a series of sculptures consisting of blocks of alabaster hollowed out through a circular or oval aperture. In each case a gentle light filters through the veined skin that remains at the back of the block. Each void seems empty, yet also to contain light as if that were a vapour. Nothing could be simpler than a piece of stone. Yet Kapoor had produced something with the aura of a tabernacle. In line with the alchemical analogy, however, there is a double meaning. On the one hand the transformation of the stone leads to the spiritual order, to a sense of a space beyond the material. On the other hand it produces something obviously sensual. One wants to touch and stroke the alabaster. Its translucence suggests life radiant within a body, and the light contained within the volume appears ethereal. The heavy has become light and the light has become spirit. Although this is not an avowedly religious work, it suggests the possibility that there may be more than matter, or at least that matter can be made graceful and we be made more gracious by observing it. Likewise in a more primitive way with the ochre pieces, and with most of what we value as great art.

According to theism we are made by and for God but we have to find our way to him, and that involves aiming ourselves towards a goal. This is the business of self-realisation: the process of becoming fully and actually what, in part and in potentiality, we already are. Herein ethics and art are conjoined. The category of the practical subsumes both the moral and aesthetic since the latter is primarily a matter of activity. To be sure, there is the aesthetic as experienced beauty: contemplation of form for its own sake. But this most commonly arises from making, and from appreciating what making expresses. For this reason the aesthetic of nature properly suggests the idea of a maker of nature. Admittedly it could be that the appearance of aesthetic order in the natural world is an illusion. The pleasing composition in the forms of living things could just be projections onto an aesthetically blank world. The possibility of a suasive design argument remains, however, if, as I have claimed, the idea of beauty is internally related to that of aesthetic design, and if, as I would also maintain, the appearances of natural beauty, recorded by people of different cultures, places and times, are as they indeed appear, namely aspects of the world.

Having recognised important connections between the moral and the aesthetic, one may reapply the alchemical analogy, now in relation to ideas of excellence in artistry and moral character. Thus one might hope that as a practitioner develops his skills, so he might want to animate them with an equal depth of informed feeling about the human condition. As and when that occurs, one might also expect the artist to look for an account of the deepest meaning of this condition. And since the most obvious candidates for providing this are those afforded by religious accounts of human nature, we should not be surprised that so many artists have been drawn to and inspired by those accounts. Thus we are returned to the idea that human reflection leads to a quest for meaning and that this search achieves its ultimate fulfilment in coming to God. That process begins in life but the questions remain of whether it may be completed there, and of what in any case is the significance of mortality. In a letter of 1787, Mozart wrote that 'death (strictly speaking) is the true ultimate purpose of our life ... and has much about it that is soothing and comforting.' In the next chapter I will consider what truth there may be in this.

7

Religion, Death and the Meaning of Life

Perhaps when we come to die, death will provide the meaning and the sequel and the ending of this adventure.
Alain-Fournier

In the summer of 2002, Ted Williams, one of America's greatest baseball heroes, died. His career had been with the Boston Red Sox, and he was especially revered there. In 1995 Boston had dedicated a $2.3 billion harbour tunnel to him, and when it became known that he had died, the groundskeepers at Fenway Park, the Red Sox stadium, shaved his 'No. 9' into the left field spot where he used to play. At the next Boston game the teams lined up, heads bowed, while a Marine Corps honour guard presented the flag. Around the country, flags in other stadiums were lowered to half mast, and silence was observed. Tributes were delivered by sportsmen, commentators, public leaders and even the President. As in ages past, a hero of the people had died and there was sadness across the nation. Williams's personal reputation was of someone ambitious and resolute, but also shy and taciturn. Obituarists generally observed that he had mellowed in later life, but even in earlier days the tendency was to excuse unsociability on grounds of greatness. In a profile of Williams, John Updike once wrote that 'Gods do not answer letters.'

It is now often said that even if, unlike gods, men are mortal and cannot hope literally to live again, nonetheless they survive in their progeny and in the memories of others. By this last measure Ted Williams may be thought to have a lifespan considerably longer than the 83 years during which warm blood coursed through his veins. It quickly transpired, however, that he, or two of his three children, may have had hopes of a more tangible future. Early press reports of his death ended with the words 'funeral arrangements were not immediately announced'. It soon emerged that no such arrangements were even in preparation. Instead, within hours of his death in Florida, the body of Ted Williams had been shipped to the Alcor Life Extension Foundation in Scottsdale, Arizona, where it had been cryonically preserved – i.e. deep-frozen with liquid nitrogen.

Immediately, sibling fighting broke out. Williams's eldest daughter claimed he had wanted to be cremated and that the freezing was part of a commercial scheme to sell his DNA; now, he would 'shatter at the touch of her finger'. Meanwhile her half-brother and sister insisted that they had no plans to profit from their father's death, but that he had changed his mind about cremation and wanted to be preserved with them so that they could later be brought back to life together. Lawyers appeared and rival documents were produced, including a singed, ink-stained note allegedly bearing Williams's signature in which he and the two children in question are said all to agree 'to be put into bio-stasis'. Sadly, the best efforts of Williams's admirers could not protect his passing from being associated with absurdity.

Whatever the truth about Ted Williams's own intentions, the fact is that a growing number of people are looking to science to save them from unending death. Some believe that current medical technology may deliver life-preserving therapies. Others place their hopes further forward in time, and plan to follow Williams in taking 'the ambulance to the future'. Commercial cryonic services began in the US in the 1970s. Clients may elect simply to have their brains frozen or they may opt for full body preservation. The remains are stored in 'cryostats', steel cylinders each able to hold four bodies with a central column also stacked with heads. Clients hope that at some point in the future when a cure for death has been found they may be reanimated, and in the case of those reduced to brains inserted into new bodies. It should go without saying that these hopes are scientifically absurd. A dead body or brain may not rot while frozen, but it is in the same position as the once-living contents of a family freezer. Ironically, the European agent for the Cryonics Institute of Detroit appears equally sceptical. A Christian, he is quoted as saying 'I think if they come back it will be on the day of resurrection'.

A couple of years ago I was due to fulfil a commitment to take part in a debate on atheism and theism in Melbourne with J.J.C. Smart, the philosopher with whom I had co-authored a book debating the same topics. This exchange was to be the centre-piece of a conference on faith and reason that had been long planned, and on which the organisers had expended much time, effort and money. As the date approached, however, my mother, who had been chronically ill and slowly failing for some years, declined further. This posed the dilemma of whether to go to Australia or to remain with her. There had been earlier occasions on which it seemed that she might die but after which she then revived. That history, together with the knowledge that my mother was being well cared for and would continue to be frequently visited by my wife and children, along with the consideration that those expecting me in Australia would have their event spoiled were the debate to be cancelled, inclined me to go ahead.

On the other hand, being an only child and close to my mother I was troubled that she might die while I was away. Having explained the position to the Australians I delayed making a decision until the last possible moment. The night before the first flight of the long journey from Scotland via France and Hong Kong to Australia, I spent some time with my mother and then set off to stay at the airport hotel in Edinburgh. In the course of that night and again the following morning I phoned to check on how things stood. She was awake and was being visited by my wife. After alerting the Australians to the fact that my stay would only be for two days (and not for the longer planned period) and checking on the possibilities of returning at any point en route, I made the difficult decision to go to Australia. In Paris I phoned back; all was well. In Hong Kong I phoned back; all was well. On arriving in Melbourne I phoned back; my mother had died, with my wife at her side.

In the *Confessions*, Augustine writes of the death of his own mother Monica: on that day 'that religious and devout soul was set free from the body.' Later he adds: 'she had not died unhappy, and she had not altogether died. Of these things – by the evidence of her virtuous life and by her "faith unfeigned", among other reasons – we felt assured.' He then recounts the prayers and rituals observed by the grieving household, leading to a funeral Mass: 'the sacrifice of your redemption was offered up unto you for her.' Augustine was fortunate in having the human comfort of knowing of Monica's virtue, the supernatural hope that she would be rewarded with the gift of eternal life, and the religious offices supportive of that hope. My own mother was a devout Catholic who practised her faith in a spirit of love rather than duty. When she could no longer attend daily and then weekly Mass she was visited by her priest who administered the sacraments. She herself hoped and prayed for the life of the world to come, believing that by God's grace she might be reunited with loved ones and enter into the company of the blessed for all eternity. In Melbourne, in St

Andrews, in London and elsewhere masses were said for the repose of her soul, both before and after her body was gently laid in a grave.

All these stories touch on human hope and other deep emotions. Thoreau (1817-62) wrote that 'the mass of men lead lives of quiet desperation.' He might as truthfully have said that most human lives are only intermittently happy, but his observation registers the presence of shadows more significant than the illumination that accompanies them, and the greatest of these shadows is the prospect of death. One of the questions I am concerned with is whether the hope of those such as my mother and the millions of others who have lived and died in the expectation of future life is any more reasonable than that of the forty or so existing cryonics clients. The answer to this depends crucially upon certain metaphysical possibilities which I shall explore in some detail. But there is also the question of whether the life hoped for, either supernaturally or naturally, is a life worth living. In the case of cryonics, the only hope is of more life; in the case of religion, the favourable prospect is of life transformed and perfected. It is not evident, however, what the latter might amount to, and this is also something I hope to get clearer about before drawing to a close. Meanwhile, it is worth reflecting on the observation of the Confucian philosopher Xun Zi (3rd century BC) that sentiments of loss for the dead, and the ritual expression of these, mark the highest point of civilisation and culture. Whatever heavenly judgment may or may not fall upon the deceased; the living are certainly measured by their grieving and by their rituals for the dead.

There are, I think, four basic possibilities for future personal life. First, while human bodies perish there may be a *material continuant* of some sort whereby the person survives as a body of a different kind. This is one way of understanding the idea of ghosts, namely as ethereal figures remaining after the demise of the gross physical body. Another, related, interpretation might suggest that what survives is the person materially transformed into a new kind of body, the corpse being a waste product of this process. It is, of course, highly disputable whether there are ethereal bodies, and even if there are, no one has an account of how the processes of bodily separation or metamorphosis might occur. Still, science admits unsolved mysteries, and the circumstances of detachment or transformation may be unique in nature, and their upshots only rarely observed by those on this side of the divide. More to the point, however, it is unclear what these possibilities would achieve so far as the overcoming of death is concerned. There is no reason to suppose that a post-human material body would be immune to injury, degradation and death. From that second ending a yet subtler body might emerge, but without some special provision this too will go the way of all flesh. The idea of someone's 'fading away' takes on a new meaning, but whether life ends in a single episode or by successive attrition the upshot is the same: eternal death.

The second possibility is that while life ends with bodily death there is a future point at which we are somehow re-created. This corresponds to one understanding of the traditional belief in resurrection. In his First Letter to the Corinthians, St Paul addresses their concern about the prospect of future life. Having reminded them of his teaching that Christ died and then rose from the dead he writes:

> But some of you will ask 'how are the dead raised? with what kind of body do they come?' You foolish man! What you sow does not come to life unless it dies. And what you sow is not the body which is to be, but a bare kernel …
> So it is with the resurrection of the body. What is sown is perishable, what is raised is imperishable. It is sown in dishonour, it is raised in glory. It is sown a physical body [*soma psuchikon*], it is raised a spiritual body [*soma pneumatikon*].

This is a memorable passage, but it is made problematic by the fact that Paul's analogy with the seed and the plant can now be seen to be doubly flawed. First, the seed comes from one living thing, while the shoot that emerges from it is another, not the old plant restored to life, but a new offspring. Second, Paul erroneously assumes that the kernel that enters the ground is dead. His assumption was common in antiquity and was connected to the ancient belief in natural rebirth. Tertullian (160-225), a convert to Christianity whose influential writings earned him the title 'Father of Latin theology', observes that 'nature teaches us to expect [our] resurrection, for if all things rise again for man ... it is absurd to think that the thing on whose account nothing perishes should itself perish entirely' (*Of the Resurrection of the Dead*). What he is appealing to is the belief that the setting and rising of the sun, the waning and waxing of the moon, the dying back and rising up of grass and plants, are all cases of things coming back to life. An ironic commentator might observe that the springtime of those who have died seems long delayed. Fortunately, however, the claim that we are restored to life by being re-created does not stand or fall on the success of the analogy of natural rebirth. This, though, focuses attention on the obscurity of Paul's idea of the resurrected person. He speaks of a spiritual body (*soma pneumatikon*), but that seems to be an oxymoron, as if one were to speak of an 'intangible solid'. If something is spiritual, how can it be a body? If it is a body, how can it be non-material? I shall return to these perplexities later.

The third possibility is that persons are not to be identified with bodies at all, but are in truth *immaterial souls* which are neither transformed nor destroyed at death, but either enter new bodies (reincarnation) or persist unembodied in some kind of spirit world. This is a familiar religious view which can be found in most cultures. The idea that souls transmigrate from one incarnation to another is usually linked, as in Buddhism and Hinduism, to a theory of moral cause and effect, and thereby to the notion of progress (or decline). When the end state of this process is taken to be release into a state of pure spirit, the upshot is a position akin to that more favoured in the West, namely the idea of immediate and permanent post-mortem disembodiment. In purely philosophical terms there is no obvious basis on which to favour one rather than the other of these two immaterial soul theories. There is said to be evidence of reincarnation in the testimony of those who claim to have witnessed events in previous lives, but apart from the reasonable doubts one may feel about such claims, even if it were the case that someone seemed to have experiences of episodes that occurred before their birth this could be explained on the other theory as telepathic communication from the disembodied souls of the deceased. I remember as a child seeing an interview with someone who claimed to have been the maidservant of the high priest Caiaphas. Such a person is described in the Gospels as approaching Peter after the Crucifixion, and identifying him as being a follower of the Nazarene. The interviewee went on to give the sort of description of the circumstances that one would only expect from someone who had witnessed them directly. This may all be nonsense. My point, however, is that even if the reported facts were true, this would not establish the identity of the interviewee with the maidservant, since it could be that the maidservant's disembodied soul was communicating her own undimmed memories through an unwitting subject.

Moreover, just as reincarnation claims to be supported

by empirical evidence, so does the thesis of disembodiment. One kind of testimony is that of mediums who report messages from those who have 'crossed over'. No doubt most of those who earn a living in this way are charlatans who skilfully play upon their audiences, but the performances of some proclaimed mediums certainly challenge the easy assumption that it is all trickery. Whether these performances refute it is another matter. Beyond the testimony of mediums, however, there is the purported evidence of out-of-body experiences. This has been the subject of recent interest in connection with the investigation of 'near-death experience'. So great is that interest that the acronym NDE is now commonly used, and there is an International Association for Near-Death Studies which publishes the *Journal of Near-Death Studies*. The common style of reports of these experiences has even become familiar to the extent of being made the subject of satire, for example in the Monty Python film *The Meaning of Life*, which shows Heaven at the end of a tunnel as an expensive hotel enlivened by a perpetual cabaret. The pattern it draws on is fairly simple. Typically, a person falls victim to some life-threatening condition. Efforts are made to save them from death, but their heart and breathing actually stop. Subsequently, circulation and ventilation are resumed and they return to consciousness. What they then report is that in the interim they were aware (sometimes from a perspective 'outside' their own bodies) of the efforts to save them and of the initial failure of these, and that following their clinical 'death' they then experienced a movement through darkness (the tunnel) to a place of light and celestial peace. Here they were greeted by guardians of the garden (and sometimes by deceased relatives). Just as their hearts filled with happiness, however, they were told that they must return to the place from whence they came. They then journeyed back through the darkness, and on the way became aware of increasing pain (accompanying their re-embodiment), after which they were revived.

As with the evidence of séances, it is easy enough to dismiss this as a combination of uncritical inference and wishful thinking, and to offer a rival account of the experiences as fantasies induced by oxygen starvation, a consequence of which is a progressive narrowing of the visual field towards its centre. This response is too quick. For one thing, the reported range of experiences is actually much greater than the tunnel type, and in many cases patients do not report visual or auditory experiences at all, but testify instead to the dawning of a sense of purpose and of general value. This latter effect bears directly on further commonly reported features – such as a subsequent decline in anxiety, often including a loss of the specific fear of death, and a change of priorities and values away from competitiveness and acquisitiveness and towards co-operation and divestment of what have come to seem worthless attachments. Less well known is the fact that NDEs bear similarities to another family of reported experiences undergone by people who are not in danger of death, namely 'transportations' to a spiritual world.

Versions of these reports may be gathered from most religious traditions. They feature in Judaism – as in the Book of Enoch compiled in the second century BCE, where the patriarch is taken up by an angel to visit a beautiful garden and then travels elsewhere to see the souls of the dead. Enoch's experience is later referred to in Paul's Letter to the Hebrews (11:5), and it is in the Second Letter to the Corinthians that we learn of his own out-of-this-world experience: 'I know a man in Christ who 14 years ago was caught up into the third Heaven – whether in the body or out of it I do not know, God knows. And I know that this man was caught up into Paradise … and he heard things that cannot be told, which man may not utter.' Notwithstanding this insistence on silence, two centuries later a Greek text entitled *The Vision of St Paul* began to circulate. This claimed to be Paul's testimony of how he came to see that human death is a moment of revelation of the state of the soul, when it is exposed for judgment preparatory to reward or condemnation. *The Vision of St Paul* became a model for the tradition of medieval 'art of death' manuals instructing people in the preparation of their souls in anticipation of divine judgment. It has also had an influence on the writings of ecstatic mystics, including several notable women writers such as Mechthild of Magdeburg (1207-82) and Catherine of Genoa (1447-1510), who reported visions of the souls in Heaven, Purgatory and Hell, experiences which in turn are related in content to those recorded by the Fatima visionaries.

Paul writes of not knowing whether his mystical journey was out of the body or with it. In light of his remarks in I Corinthians about bodily resurrection one might be inclined to suppose the latter, but that was not the received view, and Paul's own uncertainty suggests that he was willing to regard it as being a purely spiritual ecstasy. Most religious traditions include reports of mystics who were transported out of themselves, and those who give credibility to such reports generally regard them as testament to the non-materiality of mind or soul, and of its actual separability from the physical body: in short, as evidence for what has come to be known as 'substance dualism'.

The fourth possibility is that while persons are to be identified with living human bodies there is an *immaterial part* of the person which survives death and then either persists in its incompleteness, or is reincarnated, or is reunited with the original body or with some continuant of it. The reunification option provides another interpretation of the idea of resurrection, and belief in the combination of the survival of a spiritual part with its subsequent reunion with a body is common within the Eastern Orthodox and Roman Catholic traditions. This is the position advanced by Aquinas, and it explains his observation that 'I am not my soul [*anima mea non est ego*], and if only souls are saved then neither I nor any human is saved' (Commentary on I Corinthians). What he means is that people are psychosomatic unities, and that if this unity is sundered then even if something survives it cannot be the person. He thinks that there is a surviving intellect, but that this intellect is incapable of experiencing or acting on the natural world and probably incapable of remembering having done so when existing as the intellect of a living human being. Such a condition could not possibly constitute the completion of human life as we understand it; therefore – assuming there is a God to provide for this – there will be a restoration of fully personal life through bodily resurrection. Like Paul, Aquinas takes Christ's resurrection from the dead to provide a promise and a model for this.

Let me term the four basic possibilities outlined above a) *material continuation*, b) *material recreation*, c) *full immaterial continuation* and d) *partial immaterial continuation*, it being noted that reincarnation could be a version of c) or of d). Earlier I described the foregoing as the possibilities for future *personal* life, anticipating a contrast with doctrines of non-personal survival and immortality, such as the idea associated most commonly with Eastern religions that death occasions a moment of psychical dissolution into a common cosmic soul, or the return of a droplet (or flame) of mind (in Hinduism, *atman*) to the cosmic ocean (or fire) that is universal spirit (*Brahman*). I shall not discuss these ideas, in part because they involve considerable metaphysical obscurities, in part because they have little if any connection with the quest for ultimate *personal* meaning and, relatedly, because few readers of this book who hope for, or fear, the prospect of future life are likely to be concerned with this non-personal form of post-mortem existence. In setting aside ideas of non-personal immortality, however, I am not dismissing them as unworthy of attention.

Most people who believe in life after death do so as part of more general religious beliefs, or retain it as a residue of these. That is significant: it may be that the best hope of future existence depends on there being a deity to provide it. Moreover, without a religious meaning it is hard to see why surviving death or living again could be thought to have any great point or value. Before exploring this, I want to indicate how a belief in at least the possibility of life after bodily death may be warranted independently of religious assumptions. A hundred years ago, most academic philosophers in the English-speaking world subscribed to some form of mind-body dualism, believing that the thinking subject is distinct from his or her body. By the middle of the 20th century the trend was clearly away from this, and by the 1970s materialism was probably the majority view. Since then things have become more complex, as efforts to work out the details of a materialist account of mind have run into difficulties, and current opinion is somewhat confused, with virtually all possibilities having able adherents and critics.

When discussing the views of thinkers such as Dawkins, I described them as 'scientific naturalists' and explained that this is not so much a scientific theory as a philosophical one. The idea that human beings are animals and that they are composed of material particles is beyond serious dispute, but of itself it does not imply that we are nothing but material objects. If substance dualism were correct then we should disambiguate the idea of ourselves so as to distinguish between our *bodies* (what you see writing at the desk) and our *souls* (what thinks as its body writes). The fact that the composition and operation of the body is wholly describable in material terms leaves untouched the question of whether a person is identical with, or reducible to his or her body. And there are reasons for thinking that in some respects at least we do indeed transcend matter. The principal considerations involve states or activities that do not seem to be identifiable with bodily processes. First, there is the fact of phenomenal consciousness: the awareness of qualitative experiences such as those of colour, sound and odour, and of feelings of warmth and cold, pain and pleasure, etc. These features are doubly subjective: first, they are felt by subjects; and, second, they may be experienced in the absence of any corresponding objective reality. Consciousness always has a subject, but it need not have a real object (when hallucinating one may see colours and hear sounds that are not really there; an amputee may feel pain in a missing limb). Added to this oddity is the consideration that phenomenal consciousness appears to resist scientific identification. However long and hard a neurologist looks in the brain of a patient he or she will not see there the features that characterise the patient's experience. At the same time, there are obvious correlations between physical facts and subjective awareness. The radical dualist may point out that these do not even establish that experiences are dependent on physical facts, let alone that they *are* physical facts, but a more plausible position would suggest that consciousness emerges in animals of certain levels of material organisation in direct consequence of that organisation. That satisfies the intuition that awareness is something non-physical while granting that it cannot exist without a material basis. Once this is allowed, however, the possibility of awareness surviving bodily death is excluded. So far as that issue is concerned, therefore, we may as well be what the scientific naturalist supposes we are: exclusively and exhaustively material.

It might be replied that the resurrectionist possibility would still be available in the form of material recreation, and recently there has been something of a fashion among religious philosophers to favour this option. It has the appeal of providing a prospect of future life even should materialism win the debate about the nature of persons, and it also enjoys apparent scriptural support in Paul's teaching about bodily resurrection. That said, given that they believe in an immaterial deity, it is hardly open to theists to grant that materialism is the general truth about reality, and therefore there is no general philosophical gain in conceding the materiality of persons. Second, some Christian and other religious teachings also favour the idea that the souls of the deceased exist unembodied awaiting resurrection. Paul's observations in I Corinthians concerning the nature of resurrection are silent on the issue of what may precede it. Third, there is a major philosophical difficulty in the idea that life after death is provided entirely by material re-creation. This was touched on in discussion of Paul's analogy with the seed. It is the problem of identity. If a material object is destroyed and then later its matter is fashioned into an object of the same sort, we would conclude that the latter was a replica of the former and not one and the same object reconstituted. Similarly, the possibility of human material reconstitution is insufficient to allow us to say that those who died live again. It appears, therefore, that for all that the hope of future life may rest on the idea of resurrection this can only be part of the story; there also needs to be a carrier of identity across the gap between dissolution and reconstitution.

Phenomenal consciousness is of little help: first, because we have overwhelming empirical evidence to believe that it depends on a material substratum; and, second, because its contents reflect engagement with the material world. Hallucinations and phantom-limb pains are exceptions that prove the rule. The very idea of such experiences borrows from veridical cases in which what one sees, hears or smells is the result of the impact of the external world on the senses. Remove the organs of sight, hearing and so on, and their internal correlates supporting memory and imagination, and the very idea of experience falls apart. For these reasons we should consider the suggestion of the ancients and medievals that what is immaterial is not consciousness, but abstract thought. In claiming this, they were not unaware of the dependence of thought on experience; indeed the medievals coined the slogan 'there is nothing in the intellect that was not first in the sense,' but they made the important distinction between sensory patterns and concepts. It is one thing to be able to distinguish shapes on the basis of their visible differences, but quite another to be able to define geometrical figures. I noted in the previous chapter that the red ochre carvings suggest a process of mental abstraction: extracting patterns from experience and combining and repeating them in a formal design. Carried to a further stage this would lead to the intellectual study of geometry, which deals with idealised forms as objects in their own right. Intellect is the power of purely abstract thought by means of which minds are able to conceive unrealised possibilities, to engage in mathematics and to practise metaphysical speculation. In these spheres we are in contact with essences and meanings existing apart from the imperfections and irregularities of empirical objects. But these abstract domains are not any less real. On the contrary, they are more so to the extent that the 'objects' that populate them are immune to the contingencies that disrupt and ultimately destroy material things. Recalling the principle 'acting manifests being,' we may reason that whatever is capable of engaging immaterial objects must itself be an immaterial power, and whatever possesses an immaterial power must itself be an immaterial agent.

Thus we arrive at the idea of the intellect as an immaterial aspect of human persons. As such its essential operations do not involve a bodily organ (though the expressions of that power may do, as when we convey abstract thoughts through speech or writing). Accordingly, unlike phenomenal consciousness, we have no reason to think that intellect cannot survive the destruction of the body. Yet for all its power to explore the vastness of abstract domains, the life of a disembodied intellect is liable to lack much that we associate with human meaning and value. This is what Aquinas recognised, and why he reasoned that living again as a person depends on being reunited with a body. However, the argument for an intellectual soul provides an important part of a broader case against scientific materialism. It also explains how the coming to be of a human person at a time following one's death may still constitute one's own resurrection, due to the identification with each body of one and the same intellect. Beyond that it suggests a further argument for the existence of God. If mind transcends matter then matter is incapable of producing mind. Consequently, this aspect of human beings is not the result of biological reproduction or of any other material process. Being neither the effect of generation nor of modification of any previously existing stuff it can only be the product of creation *ex nihilo* – and there is only one cause capable of that: God.

This point has a great deal to tell us about the purpose of human life. If the distinguishing feature of human beings is that they are rational animals possessed of intellect, and if this feature calls for special direct creation, and is the basis of survival and the carrier of identity through disembodiment and into a possible resurrection, then it must also be a key to understanding the point of life and the likely character of the resurrected state. So far as the latter is concerned there is reason to look again at Paul's phrase 'spiritual body'. Paul had it in mind that the life of the world to come should involve a recognisably personal form of existence. Thus he would rightly think in terms of animation: of sights and sounds, of action and communication. On the other hand if the triumph over death is to be permanent, not just life *after* death but life *without* death, then the natural causes of decline and decay must be absent. When discussing the nature of evil in chapter 3, I noted that any dynamic material creation must involve perishing as well as coming to be, for the natural generation of goods is necessarily at the cost of what they replace. Death is a limiting case of natural evil, but any perfection of human life must involve the elimination of lesser evils also. Accordingly, in whatever sense the future life is 'bodily' it cannot involve the sort of material processes that sustain life in this world. It may be spatial, it may involve movement, it may be characterised by features such as sights and sounds, but it must also be non-material to the extent of not involving privation or entropy – and on this account one might think of its occupants as having, in some sense, 'spiritual bodies'.

Several faiths describe the state of future life as 'paradise'. The term comes from the Greek word '*paradeisos*' which (like the Hebrew '*pardes*') is presumed to derive from the old Persian noun '*pairi-da-za*' meaning a walled enclosure, as in a park or garden. In Hebrew scripture '*pardes*' sometimes refers to ordinary parks and gardens, but it is also used to speak of the Garden of Eden, the mythic site of human origination and then of its fall. The earliest use of 'paradise' to refer to a future state comes in Isaiah (51:3), where it is part of a promise of a fresh start for the people of Zion following their return from exile. At that point, almost through to the time of Christ, there was little Jewish interest in the idea of post-mortem existence. The Jewish hope was to pursue a life pleasing to God, and for one's progeny to enjoy the benefits promised by the Lord to those faithful to the covenant. By the first century, however, belief in future life had become common, and the Jewish historian Josephus (37-100) classifies sects in part by their beliefs and attitudes concerning it. In the New Testament, which was being written during the same period, there are only three mentions of 'Paradise'. The first comes in the words of Christ to one of the thieves crucified alongside him: 'I promise you, this day you will be with me in Paradise' (Luke 23:43). The second is in Paul's account of being caught up into the third Heaven (II Corinthians 12), and the third is in the Apocalypse of John: 'Who wins the victory? I will give him fruit from the tree of life, which grows in the Paradise of my God' (Revelation 2:7). Islam largely takes over the Christian and post-Biblical Jewish belief in an afterlife, with the Qur'an warning of the day of Judgment and the day of Resurrection leading to the permanent separation of the just and the unjust. What is here made explicit is implicit in the earlier Jewish and Christian developments: namely, that as well as a particular judgment on each soul on death, there will be a later general judgment and a collective resurrection to a common life in the world to come.

What is evident is the growing sense that an afterlife provides some sort of completion of what was begun earlier but was interrupted by death. How are we to understand this notion of completion and how is it related to the meaning of human history and of human life in general? When I discussed the idea of meta-narratives in chapter 4, I suggested that the course of human history is a religious one – a movement towards or away from God. Given the total dependence of all creation on God, there is no suspense as to whether good will triumph: God is perfect and undiminished, whatever damage creation may inflict on itself. There is, though, a very real question about where individuals direct themselves and where they end up. Creatures without intellect are not capable of profound deliberative choices, but realise their natures in the very business of living. As material beings they are also mortal with no continuing spiritual aspect. Rational animals, by contrast, are able to propose ends to themselves as individuals, and to pursue policies together in society. Thus arise issues of moral, cultural, political and religious values and goals.

It has periodically been an ambition of human beings

to integrate these values in a shared form of life. Views have differed on the manner of that integration and on its proper scope: whether to rest content with small, self-selected communities or to aspire to large, trans-generational societies. Something of both options is to be found in Judaism and in Christianity; one example of the second and larger ambition being the idea of Christendom. When Augustine sat down in Hippo (in present day Algeria) in 412 to write the *City of God*, he had it in mind that two years earlier the capital of the greatest empire of the ancient world had fallen to Goth invaders. The sack of Rome was the first capture of the city by foreigners in eight hundred years, and then and since it has been seen as marking the end of the Roman Empire. Augustine's aim was in part to respond to pagan critics who held that the fall of the city was due to the growth of Christianity and the consequent abandonment by Romans of their traditional protective deities. The critics were believers in a past golden age when Earth and Heaven were in harmony, and some Christians shared the assumption that true religious rectitude would ensure earthly glory. For them, therefore, the golden age lay in the future with the establishment of Christendom. Augustine rejects that assumption, attacking Roman ideas of glory, and subverting Christian expectations of earthly principalities. Certainly he sees history as leading somewhere, but its completion lies outside nature. God operates in history for the good of human beings, but his favour is not measured by worldly glory: 'That city in which it has been promised that we shall reign differs from this earthly city as widely as the sky from the Earth, life eternal from temporal joy, substantial glory from empty praises.'

For Augustine, therefore, we should pay little attention to the rise and fall of principalities and empires. As he puts it, 'The same God gave the throne to Constantine the Christian, and also to Julian the Apostate ... if God's reasons are inscrutable, does that mean they are unjust?' If this tells against the sort of view espoused by Pat Robertson that interprets the events of 11 September in terms of God's displeasure with America, it does not imply that we should not look to history to discover truths about the human condition. But these have to do with the sacred order and with the effects of a human disruption of creation. The darkening of the intellect and the disturbance of the passions are all too evident throughout the world. What, though, of the *meaning* of history? For Augustine there is a pattern to be seen. It is that recorded in scripture: creation, fall, covenant, lapse, recovenant, relapse, salvation. But this pattern is not imposed on us from some cosmic source, as in certain metaphysical theories of recurrence in which our fates are predetermined. Rather it has emerged out of the human soul, originating in free choice but resulting in habituated sinfulness. That pattern of beginning, rising and falling can be seen in the affairs of nations and empires and, more importantly, in the lives of all men and women. We can see it operating in ourselves as we set out to act well in pursuit of higher values, and then fall back into baseness.

The fact of this pattern can hardly be denied. What is at issue is its significance, both in respect of its meaning and of its ultimate consequence. The atheist may take a secularised version of it to be a brute fact, or appeal for an explanation to genetics, or evolution, or economic forces, or industrialisation, or food additives, and so on; but none of these really seems to capture the pervasiveness of the phenomenon, its involvement with the human will, or the sense that it points to a transcendent destiny. Religion as I have been concerned with it offers both an explanation and a solution. I quote again from Augustine's opening to the *Confessions*: 'Man being part of your creation desires to praise you – man who carries with him his mortality, the witness of his sin … for you have formed us for yourself; and our hearts are restless until they find their rest in you.'

However the blessed may be related to one another in paradise, their primary orientation is towards God, on whom they actively gaze, seeing in the divine nature their own source and the perfection of every positive quality. (In this connection it is worth noting the distinction between contemplation and meditation, and the fact that whereas Western religions tend to favour the former, Eastern religions are inclined to the latter. Unlike meditation, which may involve self-contained mental states, contemplation is necessarily directed upon some object, fact or supposition.) In this the intellectual powers of the blessed are fully realised, but not in a purely speculative mode. Rather, in finding what they have always craved – absolute, unconditional, and everlasting love – their minds are themselves made loving, but now without prospect of relapse, for the wound from which their darkness and disturbance issued as a consequence of wilful disobedience has now been healed, and their lives transfigured. The idea that this state might induce tedium is a product of too low an expectation of what the transformation of human life in Heaven might involve. God knows infinities by creating them; created minds know unending depths by exploring them. Even given eternity, that exploration will not be completed: as with the number series, however long one continues, and however far one reaches, there is still an infinity ahead. Those who find no attraction in the propect of unlimited exploration of a reality that is at once *significant* (in the manner of a meaning-bestowing narrative), *pleasing* (after the fashion of an aesthetically engaging composition), and *sustaining* (as in a loving friendship) are, I suggest, gravely wanting in imagination.

What, then, of those whose lives on Earth are ones of resistance to the call of God, who dig deeper into the darkness and in consequence come to hate the light and to fear the prospect of it? Most religions recognise the fact of spiritual evil, and some believe that provision is made for it in the divine scheme of things. Protestant Christians have long been dismissive of the idea of Purgatory as lacking indisputable scriptural warrant, while many contemporary Christians now reject even the idea of Hell (though they face the opposite problem of denying what is patently part of Biblical tradition). Both attitudes strike me as failing to take the measure of human deeds. So far as the idea of Purgatory is concerned it suffices, I think, to quote the words of Dr Johnson (1709-84) when Boswell asked his view:

[Catholics] are of the opinion that the generality of mankind are neither so obstinately wicked as to deserve everlasting punishment, nor so good as to merit being admitted into the society of the blessed spirits; and therefore that God is graciously pleased to allow of a middle state, where they may be purified by certain degrees of suffering. You see, Sir, there is nothing unreasonable in this.

What of those who may be 'so obstinately wicked as to deserve everlasting punishment'? A common objection to the idea of Hell is that a good God could not inflict or allow eternal suffering. This, however, rests on, at best, a partial conception of the situation. The active verb 'to damn' encourages us to think about the agency of God in the matter, but I believe that this is the wrong place to look. If there are damned, then they are such not because of what God has chosen to do to them, but because of what they have made of themselves. The kind of evil that is beyond purification is that which has so transformed the soul that it does not seek salvation and resists the measures provided to mankind for its perfection.

Someone might respond that surely God can change such a soul so as to fit it for Heaven. This is doubly flawed: first, because I am envisaging a state of being so profoundly corrupt that there is nothing left to purify; and second, because justice baulks at the idea that nothing one does can deny one a place in Heaven. I used the image of digging further into the dark and so coming to hate the light, as might one in retreat from exposure of his or her wrongdoings. Another image is that of a being so corrupted and transformed by disease that there is no good flesh, bone or blood remaining in which healing can take hold. It is a terrible thought to contemplate that we might become so bad that we would could not, and would not want to be, purified, and would even subvert efforts to achieve this in spite of ourselves. But it is that possibility of radical refusal that the idea of Hell provides for. God does not inflict damnation, but, as in the case of Heaven, he provides eternal completion for a process begun on Earth. An intelligent person interested in what religion has to say about the meaning of life should take these possibilities very seriously and recognise that if they are real then nothing could be more important than orienting oneself towards God and praying for grace. If what I have argued is correct, there is no reason to hope for personal transcendence other than on a theistic basis; but on that basis there is reason to look forward in hope to an eternity of perpetual happiness.

8

Religion and the Doubting Philosophers

Man is by his constitution a religious animal;
atheism is against not only our reason, but our instincts.
Edmund Burke

In the previous chapters I have described, interpreted and evaluated various religious phenomena and ideas, and argued that not only is religion not dwindling to small sects striving to resist a worldwide secular culture, but also that its claims should not be dismissed by an intelligent person. Yet I am conscious that among academics in fields once particularly sympathetic to religion, especially philosophy, attitudes are at best mixed, and at least among the most prominent philosophers there is scepticism as to the claims of traditional religion so far as they bear on any supernatural reality.

Why that should be is an interesting question. It will not do to take it as grounds for presuming that religion has been widely refuted, since many philosophers are simply silent on the matter, and if pressed would more likely express themselves agnostic rather than confidently atheist. That may be the key. For it is often said that religious claims 'go beyond' what can rationally be asserted or denied. This was formerly advanced in connection with the idea that the meaning of a statement is equivalent to the conditions of its verification. That is a philosopher's way of saying that nothing has factual content save what can be given wholly in experience, or demonstrated fully in some piece of formal reasoning. Famously, however, this account of meaning was mortally embarrassed by the fact that it transcends what can be confirmed in experience or demonstrated by reasoning. Probably nothing conceived in philosophy ever wholly dies, but if verificationism has not given up the ghost it has certainly been abandoned by the living.

Still, the influence of powerful ideas may survive their demise. Those who recall it having been said that religious claims are meaningless, and whose interests may not have encouraged them to think about this further, are likely to remain under the influence of that idea. Just the same verificationism, however, would put paid to claims about the significance of history, the meaning of life, and the value of art. One might think, therefore, that philosophers' deep concern with these matters would have caused them to fashion more accommodating theories of meaning, and then perhaps to notice that these are also welcoming to the meaningfulness of religious and theological claims. (Which is not to say that they show them to be true.) To an extent some have indeed traced this path, and the philosophy of religion thrives today in a way it did not half a century ago. But the fact is that many philosophers either take the same attitude of scepticism or agnosticism to the meaning of history, life and value; or they simply take no interest in them.

This last tendency reveals a change in the education and culture of philosophers. Once they were nurtured in the practice of religion, and then in the study of classical literature and culture, and in a later period made familiar with modern literature, history and some arts. Now it is more common for philosophers to come from a background in empirical sciences, psychology and mathematics. Of itself, there is no necessity that this change of formation should lead to a loss of interest in religion, culture and the arts. But in part because specialisation, particularly early on, means that one cannot do everything, and in part because the practice of the natural and human sciences and of mathematics is closer to the ideal of the verificationist understanding of what can be a subject of knowledge, the trend has been away from interest in or sympathy for religion.

There are, however, notable exceptions: philosophers well-schooled in abstract and theoretical aspects of the subject, who nonetheless engage matters of broader human meaning and have given time to the general question of the status of religion. It is easy enough to name major philosophers, whose reputations extend beyond the profession, and who are believers: most prominently, perhaps, Alasdair MacIntyre, Charles Taylor, Saul Kripke and Hilary Putnam. (The first and second are Roman

Catholics, the third and fourth are Jews.) It is more apt, however, to consider the reflections of two deeply humanistic thinkers who have addressed the subject of religion but failed to embrace it.

The first is Roger Scruton, author of many fine books including the excellent *Intelligent Person's Guide to Philosophy* (1996; reissued 2002). Chapter 7 bears the simple title 'God'. There he mentions Weber's notion of disenchantment, having earlier argued that one effect of natural science has been to strip the world bare of meanings, purposes and values. His complaint, quite properly, is not with science *per se* but with *scientism* – the universal application of a reductionist view to all aspects of human experience and to the human subject itself. Although he does not mention Husserl, his response is analogous to that of the great phenomenologist, reclaiming lost ground on behalf of the life-world of experience and affective response.

All this is welcome, but, as one reads on, the question begins to prey: does Scruton suppose that the enchantment he is proposing is a reality, or a projected construction serving to insulate us from a world too empty and cold to contemplate, let alone to endure? His attitude to Nietzsche is somewhat ambivalent: on the one hand recognising the importance of his concerns and the seriousness of his thoughts, on the other dismissing Nietzsche's rejection of truth as being self-refuting: 'There are no truths, said Nietzsche, only interpretations. Logic cries out against this remark. For is it true? Well, only if there are no truths.' But then he adds that Nietzsche was a genius, a great writer 'and one of the few who have peered into the abyss and recorded, in the brief moment of sanity that then remains, just how it looks'. Scruton offers something of a mixed message, leaving one wondering whether the abyss was a figment of Nietzsche's wild imagination, a description of how things would be if they were not (happily) otherwise, or an endorsement of a vision of how they really are.

Scruton's discussion of 'God' is critical in resolving this ambiguity. For there it should be clear whether he thinks the world is as Nietzsche took it to be, or whether it is as I have represented it: a creation *ex nihilo*, in which we can find real order, meaning, value and purpose, all leading into a real eternity in which we may share in the life of God. Scruton observes the importance and urgency of the task of understanding the nature and significance of religion, 'the force which once held our world together'. He writes:

A sacred place is one in which personality shines from mere objects: from a piece of stone, a tree, or a patch of water. Such things have no subjectivity [personal nature] of their own: which is why they convey the sense of God's presence …

This ability to see the world in personal terms overcomes human estrangement. It arises from a superfluity of social feeling, when the experience of membership overflows into nature, and fills it with a human animation. It confirms our freedom by providing the mirror in which freedom can be seen.

This is beautifully expressed, but it is ambiguous between the claim that we are warranted in seeing in things an expression of the being of a transcendent divinity, and the suggestion that the sacred is a sentiment of approbation arising in the human breast and then poured out over rocky ground, forming pools in which what we see are our own reflected images. If the latter, then a new disenchantment threatens as we recognise that the treatment for the sense of alienation in a meaningless world involves an illusion of objectivity. And with this we are returned to the philosophies of Hume, Nietzsche and Camus in which value is made and not found. It is as if Scruton is spiritually attracted to religion but cannot make an unambiguous commitment to it.

In the year following Scruton's *Intelligent Person's Guide*, the American philosopher Thomas Nagel published *The Last Word*. This is a sustained attack on relativism and subjectivism including the forms of these favoured by postmodernists. Nagel's strategy is akin to that worked by Scruton against Nietzsche. Those who deny that there is objective reality, or that reasoning is universally valid, are undone by the fact that in stating their negative claims they have to presuppose a framework of truth and valid inference. Thus reason has 'the last word'. Nagel also scorns the relativist's effort to reduce rationality to a form of evolved social interaction. For the objectivity of norms is presupposed in the use of language, the making of plans, the co-ordination of effort and so on. And since reason is a defining attribute of mind the issue now arises of the place of mind in a material world. How can mere matter have given rise to beings that can understand both the material universe and the abstract domains of logic and ethics? The harmonious correspondence, to which science aspires, between the way we represent the world and the way it actually is, itself appears to lie beyond scientific explanation. That suggests an argument to design.

Nagel is clearly reluctant to follow this reasoning, viewing its conclusions as admitting an unwelcome spectre, and confessing to 'a fear of religion'. Writing in obviously tendentious terms, he insists that this fear is nothing so superficial as 'the entirely reasonable hostility to certain established religions and religious institutions, in virtue of their objectionable moral doctrines, social policies and political influence … the association … with superstition and the acceptance of evident empirical falsehoods'. It is instead 'something much deeper – namely the fear of religion itself'. In an interesting suggestion he speculates that a similar fear underlies the commitment of many philosophers who favour reductionist and scientistic approaches, but he argues that it is possible to resist reductionism without embracing theism:

If the natural order can include universal, mathematically beautiful laws of fundamental physics of the kind we have discovered, why can't it include equally fundamental laws and constraints that we don't know anything about, that are consistent with the laws of physics and that render intelligible the development of conscious organisms some of which have the capacity to discover ... some of the fundamental truths about that very natural order? ... the possibility [of the existence of mind] must be explained. And it seems hardly credible that its appearance should be a natural accident, like the fact that there are mammals.

One may ask why the existence of (mere) mammals may be a 'natural accident' whereas the existence of thinkers must be explained. While not doubting that mindedness calls for an explanation, one might also suppose that non-rational animals also exhibit purposeful behaviour and that this points more directly to an agent of design. Such indeed is the substance of Aquinas's 'fifth way' as set out in the *Summa Theologiae*:

> We see that things which lack knowledge, such as natural bodies, act for an end ... Now whatever lacks knowledge cannot move towards an end unless it be directed by some being endowed with knowledge and intelligence; as the arrow is directed by the archer. Therefore some intelligent being exists by whom all natural things are directed to their end; and this we call 'God'.

We have already considered the idea that arguments of this sort are untenable in light of evolutionary theory. I will not pursue this again now, but refer interested readers to the previously mentioned debate between J.J.C. Smart and myself. I note, however, that since Nagel rejects the idea that the rational order exhibited by mindedness can be given an evolutionary explanation it is then not open to him to meet an argument from ordered rationality to design by saying that order is only ever apparent and not real. More interesting in this context, though, is his resistance to the idea of creation on the grounds that he does not want it to be true. 'It isn't just that I don't believe in God. It is that I hope there is no God! I don't want there to be a God, I don't want the universe to be like that.'

It is unclear exactly what the grounds of Nagel's aversion are, but there are a couple of clues. First, the next sentence begins: 'My guess is that this cosmic authority problem is not a rare condition.' What looked as if it might be a theoretical issue to do with the idea of a deity having a purpose in creating a world such as ours now seems to have become an existential problem with accepting that our lives might be under the governance of and answerable to the authority of such a creator. Second, at an earlier place in the book Nagel anticipates his later theme:

How is it possible for finite beings like us to think infinite thoughts? … a well-known answer is the religious one: the universe is intelligible to us because it and our minds were made for each other … I have never been able to understand the idea of God well enough to see such a theory as truly explanatory: it seems rather to stand for a still unspecified purposiveness that itself remains unexplained. But perhaps this is due to my inadequate understanding of religious concepts.

Although Nagel is a very able philosopher I suspect that from what little he says about theism that he has indeed simply not given enough thought to this perspective. It is a mystery that there are thinkers whose minds engage the structure of reality, and follow rules of reason. In antiquity the first philosophers were moved by contemplation of these same facts to posit a universal intellectual principle governing the universe, *Nous* (Mind) whose expression is *logos* (word). Half a millennium later, John the Evangelist, a Greek-speaking Jew, sat down to write of how the *logos* that the Greeks sought had entered the world: 'In the beginning was the *logos* and the *logos* was with God, and the *logos* was God.' What John and his readers were attracted to, Nagel is repelled by. I find this genuinely puzzling and even wayward. Religion offers an account that is subtle, deep and serious. But in revealing us to be creatures of a purposeful deity it also forces us to ask questions about our nature, our responsibilities and our destiny. Perhaps Nagel's own final words may yet be directed to God, but in contrast to Scruton his present resistance strikes me as more spiritual than intellectual. It may be less a matter of not understanding the religious answer than of not wanting to consider it for fear of what it may reveal.

This returns me to the most promising but also the most mysterious aspect of theism: the idea that, like children in process of education, we exist for a reason not yet fully revealed or attained but one in which we may participate as beneficiaries. I have speculated about what the life of the world to come might involve, and why it would constitute a completion. If theism is correct, however, we need and should not remain passively awaiting our deaths to reveal our future lives. For it is the teaching of all the great religions that the journey to eternity has already begun and that those who would hope to complete it must make sure to walk in the right path now. For that a 'guide' may be necessary, but if so it will have to be another one than this.

Further Reading

The following includes some items already quoted from or referred to, plus a few others which may be helpful to readers wishing to pursue the themes discussed in this book.

General

Markham, I. (ed.), *A World Religions Reader*, 2nd Edition (Blackwell 2000)

Hinnells, J. R. (ed.), *A Handbook of Living Religions* (Penguin 1988)

Smart, N. and Hecht, R.D. (eds), *Sacred Texts of the World*: *A Universal Anthology* (Macmillan 1982)

Corrigan, J. et al., *Jews, Christians, Muslims*: *A Comparative Introduction to Monotheistic Religions* (Prentice Hall 1998)

Wansbrough, H. (ed.), *The New Jerusalem Bible* (Oxford University Press 1990)

Metzger, B. and Coogan, M., *The Oxford Companion to the Bible* (Oxford University Press 1993)

de Lange, N., *Judaism* (Oxford University Press 1987)

Johnson, P., *A History of Christianity* (Penguin 1990)

Waines, D., *An Introduction to Islam* (Cambridge University Press 1995)

Flood, G.D., *An Introduction to Hinduism* (Cambridge University Press 1996)

Ching, J., *Chinese Religions* (Macmillan 1993)

Keown, D., *Buddhism: A Very Short Introduction* (Oxford University Press 1996)

Grant, M. (ed.), *Readings in the Classical Historians* (Scribner 1992)

Morgan, M.L. (ed.), *Classics of Moral and Political Theory* (Hackett 1992)

Particular

Arnold, M., *Selected Poems and Prose*, ed. M. Allcott (Dent 1983)

Augustine, *City of God*, trans. H. Bettenson (Penguin 1991)

Augustine, *Confessions*, trans. H. Chadwick (Oxford University Press 1998)

Aquinas, *Selected Philosophical Writings*, trans. and ed. Timothy McDermott (Oxford University Press 1998)

Badham, P., *Christian Beliefs about Life After Death* (Macmillan 1976)

Behe, M., *Darwin's Black Box: The Biochemical Challenge to Evolution* (Free Press 1996)

Camus, A., *The Myth of Sisyphus*, trans. J. O'Brien (Hamish Hamilton 1965)

Coomaraswamy, A.K., *Christian and Oriental Philosophy of Art* (Dover 1956)

Dawkins, R., *River out of Eden* (Weidenfeld & Nicolson 1995)

Freud, S., *The Future of an Illusion*, trans. J. Strachey (W.W. Norton 1961)

Fukuyama, F., *The End of History and the Last Man* (Penguin 1992)

Graham, G., *The Shape of the Past: A Philosophical Approach to History* (Oxford University Press 1997)

Hegel, G.W.F., *The Philosophy of History*, trans. J. Sibree (Wiley 1956)

Hegel, G.W.F., *The Phenomenology of Spirit*, trans. A.V. Miller (Oxford University Press 1977)

Hume, D., *Treatise of Human Nature*, 2nd Edition, edited by L.A. Selby-Bigge, revised by P.H. Nidditch (Oxford University Press 1978)

Hume, D. *The Natural History of Religion and Dialogues Concerning Natural Religion*, eds A.W. Glyn and J.V. Price (Oxford University Press 1976)

Husserl, E., *The Crisis of European Sciences and Transcendental Phenomenology*, trans. D. Carr (Northwestern University Press 1970)

Lyotard, J.-F., *The Postmodern Condition*, trans. G. Bennington & B. Massumi (Manchester University Press 1992)

Martin, J.A., *Beauty and Holiness: The Dialogue Between Aesthetics and Religion* (Princeton University Press 1990)

Nagel, T., *The Last Word* (Oxford University Press 1997)

Nietzsche, F., *Basic Writings*, trans. and ed. Walter Kaufmann (New York 1992)

Panofsky, E., *Gothic Architecture and Scholasticism* (Meridian 1976)

Scruton, R., *An Intelligent Person's Guide to Philosophy* (Duckworth 1996 and 2002)

Smart, J.J.C. and Haldane, J.J., *Atheism and Theism*, 2nd Edition (Blackwell 1996, 2nd Edition 2003)

Williams, B., *Truth and Truthfulness* (Princeton University Press, 2002)

Wilson, A.N., *God's Funeral* (John Murray 1999)

Zaleski, C., *Otherworld Journeys: Accounts of Near-Death Experience in Medieval and Modern Times* (Oxford University Press 1987)

Index

INDEX